AlterNatives

CULTURAL SURVIVAL STUDIES
IN ETHNICITY AND CHANGE SERIES

Allyn and Bacon

David Maybury-Lewis and Theodore Macdonald, Jr., Series Editors
Cultural Survival, Inc., Harvard University

Malaysia and the "Original People": A Case Study of the Impact of Development on Indigenous Peoples by Robert Knox Dentan, Kirk Endicott, Alberto G. Gomes, and M. B. Hooker
Order No. 0-205-19817-1

Gaining Ground? Evenkis, Land, and Reform in Southeastern Siberia by Gail A. Fondahl
Order No. 0-205-27579-6

Ariaal Pastoralists of Kenya: Surviving Drought and Development in Africa's Arid Lands by Elliot Fratkin
0-205-26997-4

Ethnicity and Culture amidst New "Neighbors": The Runa of Ecuador's Amazon Region by Theodore Macdonald, Jr.
Order No. 0-205-19821-X

Indigenous Peoples, Ethnic Groups, and the State, Second Edition by David Maybury-Lewis
Order No. 0-205-33746-5

Aboriginal Reconciliation and the Dreaming: Warramiri Yolngu and the Quest for Equality by Ian S. McIntosh
Order No. 0-205-29793-5

Defending the Land: Sovereignty and Forest Life in James Bay Cree Society by Ronald Niezen
Order No. 0-205-27580-X

Forest Dwellers, Forest Protectors: Indigenous Models for International Development by Richard Reed
Order No. 0-205-19822-8

AlterNatives: Community, Identity, and Environmental Justice on Walpole Island by Robert M. VanWynsberghe
Order No. 0-205-34952-8

AlterNatives:

Community, Identity, and Environmental Justice on Walpole Island

Robert M. VanWynsberghe
University of British Columbia

Allyn and Bacon
Boston • London • Toronto • Sydney • Tokyo • Singapore

Series Editor: Jennifer Jacobson
Series Editorial Assistant: Tom Jefferies
Marketing Manager: Judeth Hall
Cover Designer: Joel Gendron
Editorial-Production Service: Omegatype Typography, Inc.
Electronic Composition: Omegatype Typography, Inc.

ISBN: 0-205-34952-8

Printed in the United States of America

10 9 8 7 6 5 4 3 2 1   06 05 04 03 02 01

Contents

Foreword to the Series

Cultural Survival is an organization founded in 1972 to defend the human rights of indigenous peoples, who are those, like the Indians of the Americas, who have been dominated and marginalized by peoples different from themselves. Since the states that claim jurisdiction over indigenous peoples consider them aliens and inferiors, they are among the world's most underprivileged minorities, facing a constant threat of physical extermination and cultural annihilation. This is no small matter, for indigenous peoples make up approximately five percent of the world's population. Most of them wish to become successful ethnic minorities, meaning that they be permitted to maintain their own traditions even though they are out of the mainstream in the countries where they live. Indigenous peoples hope therefore for multiethnic states that will tolerate diversity in their midst. In this their cause is the cause of ethnic minorities worldwide and is one of the major issues of our times, for the vast majority of states in the world are multiethnic. The question is whether states are willing to accept and live peaceably with ethnic differences, or whether they will treat them as an endless source of conflict.

Cultural Survival works to promote multiethnic solutions to otherwise conflictive situations. It sponsors research, advocacy and publications which examine situations of ethnic conflict, especially (but not exclusively) as they affect indigenous peoples, and suggests solutions for them. It also provides technical and legal assistance to indigenous peoples and organizations.

This series of monographs entitled "Cultural Survival Studies on Ethnicity and Change Series" is published in collaboration with Allyn and Bacon (the Pearson Education Group). It will focus on problems of ethnicity in the modern world and how they affect the interrelations between indigenous peoples, ethnic groups and the state.

The studies will focus on the situations of ethnic minorities and of indigenous peoples, who are a special kind of ethnic minority, as they try to defend their rights, their resources and their ways of life within modern states. Some of the volumes in the series will deal with general themes, such as ethnic conflict, indigenous rights, socioeconomic development or multiculturalism. These volumes will contain brief case studies to illustrate their general arguments. Meanwhile, the series as a whole plans to publish a larger number of books that deal in depth with specific cases. It is our conviction that good case studies are essential for a better understanding of issues that arouse such passion in the world today, and this series will provide them. Its emphasis nevertheless will be on relating the particular to the general in the comparative contexts of national or international affairs.

The books in the series will be short, averaging 100 to 150 pages in length, and written in a clear and accessible style aimed at students and the general reader. They are intended to clarify issues that are often obscure or misunderstood and that are not treated succinctly elsewhere. It is our hope, therefore, that they will also prove useful as reference works for scholars, activists and policy makers.

DAVID MAYBURY-LEWIS
THEODORE MACDONALD, JR.
Cultural Survival, Inc.
215 Prospect St.
Cambridge, Massachusetts 02139
(617) 441-5400 fax: (617) 441-5417

Foreword

We have had many visitors to Walpole Island since the French "discovered us" in the seventeenth century in our Territory, Bkejwanong. In many cases, these visitors failed to recognize who we were and to appreciate our traditions. They tried to place us in their European framework of knowledge, denying that we possessed our own indigenous knowledge. They attempted to steal our lands, waters, and knowledge. We resisted. They left and never came back. We continued to share our knowledge with the next visitors to our place, out of a spirit of mutual respect and trust. It was a long-term strategy that has lasted more than three hundred years.

In the late twentieth century, things began to change in our relationships with visitors. It was our initiative to greet them on terms of equality as human beings. We hoped that they, in turn, would reciprocate and share their knowledge with us. In doing so, we hoped that one day we could develop partnerships with individuals and organizations that had taken the time to come and share their knowledge with us on our terms. One of these individuals is Professor Edmund Danziger, who teaches history at Bowling Green State University, Ohio. Many times over the years Professor Danziger came and worked with us on projects of mutual concern. Most importantly, he began to bring his students to visit us as well. One of these students was Robert M. VanWynsberghe who came in the mid-1990s as a doctoral student. He came to Nin.Da.Waab.Jig, our Heritage Centre, and listened to us and our ways.

Our Heritage Centre has always been a community-based research group and more recently has been involved with co-operative research initiatives. Our work has been recognized locally, regionally, nationally, and internationally. We have long sought to transfer this attention to the surrounding waters (our lifeline and reason for being here). We are dedicated to protecting Mother Earth and defending our future. The community (place) has survived, but the struggles continue. Like persistent chemicals that never fade away, neither will we—we will never give up. We are persistent, and we are not going away from our place.

I am pleased to be able to write this foreword for Robert M. VanWynsberghe's book *AlterNatives: Community, Identity, and Environmental Justice on Walpole Island.* His book describes our attempts over the years to gain environmental justice and advocacy for our lands and waters. Professor VanWynsberghe has given us, in this book, the shared knowledge based on our partnership over the last decade. The author came to our place, as he describes it, armed with powerful theories. And yet, they and he were changed by his encounter with the indigenous knowledge of the citizens of the Bkejwanong. He has grasped the significance of our place as a very special place in Anishinabe history—as the soul of Indian Territory.

DR. DEAN JACOBS
Executive Director
Nin.Da.Waab.Jig
Walpole Island First Nation

Preface

The main objective of this book is to provide a detailed account of how the Walpole Island First Nation has effectively organized itself in order to protect meaningful cultural and economic ties to its natural resources. This account focuses on the Heritage Centre, a Walpole Island First Nation government body that has a twenty-year history of engaging in multifaceted endeavors to safeguard the environment. To call it an instrument of either White or Aboriginal[1] power is to reveal the tension that has dogged the Heritage Centre's efforts. I discovered that the Walpole Island Heritage Centre gains local support by representing the community's cultural values.

My research was conducted against the backdrop of the environmental justice movement and its attempt to forge links with Native populations. Environmental justice

> refers to those cultural norms and values, rules, regulations, behaviors, policies, and decisions to support sustainable communities where people can interact with confidence that their environment is safe, nurturing, and productive.... These are the communities where both cultural and biological diversity are respected and highly re-

---

1. In this book, the term *race* is used to refer to the social construction of categories of difference between populations of people. *Race* is usually fused with *"race,"* which here refers to a biological or physical category. I argue, strongly, against the conflation of *race* and *"race."* Race is a taken-for-granted factor in social identity, and we perceive racial identities according to easily recognizable physical differences (e.g., skin color). "Race" does not exist; the effects of "racism" does.

vered and where distributed justice prevails. (Bryant 1995, 5)

The efforts to form links between the environmental justice movement and Native peoples have to overcome several obstacles, including mutual suspicion, competing agendas, and covert racism (Gedicks 1993).

European settlers and Natives had very different views about agriculture, hunting, and land stewardship. These differences continue to inform Native struggles against the interests of capital, and this sometimes involves mainstream environmental groups. As Dowie (1996, 148) relates:

> After being pushed onto barren reservations by governments sympathetic to ranchers, miners, and loggers, Native Americans thought they had seen all the callous discrimination and insensitivity they could imagine. They were shocked then, when, two centuries later, white environmentalists took positions that jeopardized their survival.

Native ties to their traditions and the natural world have been unceasingly disrupted by the forces of capitalism and modernity, among which must be included many self-proclaimed environmentalists. Drawing upon the status of Native people as innate environmentalists, a certain timeless quality is attached to Native people that detaches from the here and now of mainstream society (Buege 1996). I am saying that this is a form of domination that places Native people into the past and denies them a contemporary presence. The point is that disruptions to Native communities follow these perceptions, ones that contribute to what LaDuke (1993) calls "industrialism's struggle to dominate the natural world."

Before one can include the struggles of Native communities within the framework of environmental justice, one must acknowledge "the experience of colonialism, and the imminent endangerment of [Native] culture" (Krauss 1994, 267). This point has been emphasized by Native communities that have served as literal dumpsites for capital—a situation that has led Bullard (1994, 17) to coin the term *garbage imperialism*. Garbage imperialism is generally seen as a continuation of genocidal policies directed against Native lands and culture.

Environmental threats to Native communities entail deep, species-level cultural implications. It has been argued that there can be no distinction between the goal of sustainable development and the goal of maintaining cultural diversity: "[There is] a growing political tendency within Native communities and within the mainstream and grassroots environmental movement, a tendency that sees the integral connection between Native struggles for cultural survival and struggles to protect the natural world." Furthermore, indigenous cultures are crucial to biological and cultural diversity because they are an important source of genetic diversity (La Duke 1992).

O'Connor (1993) maintains that, at the community level, traditional Native values can offer a fundamental basis for maintaining a clean environment. This being the case, alliances between Native communities and environmental justice advocates can be mutually beneficial. Gedicks (1993, 9) concurs:

> We need to join and build the Native-environmentalist alliance today and struggle for a more just, more sustainable, more desirable world. We need to integrate social information into a wider framework of restoring Earth; we need long range ecological integrity wherein the wilderness provides impetus.

At the community level, the priority for Native peoples is, of course, to determine what a Native environmental justice movement can do for them. My conclusions at this stage can only be provisional, but, based on my research to date, the utility of the environmental justice movement to Native communities lies in the space forged by the meaning that non-Natives attach to Native peoples' relationship to the non-human world.

This meaning has two elements: (1) a certain notion of history and (2) a certain image of Native peoples. I agree with Sider (1993) that history is a cognitive feat rather than an experience. Myth or circumstance may provide the roots of one's notion of history, for what is important is not so much verisimilitude as narrative consistency. Native peoples have recognized, over the 100-year history of the mainstream environmental movement, that they can partially counteract a history of oppression by focusing on a "new" history—one that, in defiance of modern cultural currents, focuses on their continued relationship to the nonhuman world.

Francis (1992, 58) maintains that many environmentalists view Native peoples as "the new Vanishing American (Indian), the Indian as spiritual and environmental guru, threatened by the forces of consumer culture." Francis asserts that these forces, the profit-seeking entities that have inundated us with books and films celebrating the spiritual side of "Indian" life, have ironically acted to symbolically annihilate Native peoples. I agree with Francis's assessment: the popularity of these items is a reflection of the desire of non-Natives to project onto Native lives the value and sense of sacredness missing in their own. As a result, yesterday's "noble savage" has become today's "ecological Native." This stereotype, according to Hale (1995, 434) and drawing on both Francis and Hornborg (1994), is:

> how Indians and whites present themselves to each other. Indians come to adopt the white man's image of Indians in order to claim authentic ethnicity in relations with white society.

Consider, for example, the famous anti-pollution advertisement of the 1970s, which featured actor Iron Eyes Cody as a traditional Native chief (and, therefore, innate environmentalist). He is photographed staring over litter in a ditch near a highway, a tear beginning to roll down his cheek. Clearly, the myth of the ecological Native, like other related cultural artifacts, affects how Natives and non-Natives promote and project themselves to each other.

The key to Native environmental justice coalitions is oppositional power, what Sider (1993, 99) describes as the "capacity of a dominated people to attack their domination precisely in its own terms and with its own symbols." The non-Native conception of Native peoples' organic and intimate relationship with the environment as an intrinsic element of Native peoples identity is a source of oppositional power for Native people. This identity can, as the example of Walpole Island shows, help us to experience grievous environmental injustices as an intolerable contradiction that cannot persist. One of the examples that I will use to document this point concerns the community's decision to reject a water pipeline as a short-term remedy for polluted river water. The reasons for this rejection amounted to Walpole's making it clear to outsiders that it is the sources of toxic contamination and not their symptoms that are its organizational focus. In short then, how Walpole Island fashions contradictions in order to resist corporate efforts to pollute its community is the substance of this book. The cultivation of the notion of the "ecological Native" helps to promote social movements on Walpole Island. It does this based, in part, on mainstream notions of ethnic groups—notions whose reproduction supports racist discourses by locating minority identity within the modern ideology of ethnicity (Nagel 1996). Like Nagel, this book is not concerned with determining the extent to which renewed traditions reflect historically authentic practices; rather, my concern is to understand the solidarity fostered by the process of inventing or renewing tradition within the context of a social movement.

My intention is to open up a dialogue regarding the prevalence of this stereotype, both for those who perpetuate and those who challenge it (e.g., students of environmentalism). This book is part of an emerging conversation about the impact of history, hegemony, and political opportunity on the construction of the notion of the ecological Native. Although certainly relevant to them, this book is not specifically designed for professional social theorists. I also intend to alert the educated lay reader to what a new understanding of how individuals construct and reflect historical and cultural particularities. What I offer is a full-blown case study that carefully analyzes the complex social dynamics involved in understanding why people invest tremendous amounts of their time and energy to ensure that their families and communities are safe from harm caused by environmental degradation.

Intent and Significance

The view from the Algonac customs pier in Michigan evokes familiar thoughts in me—thoughts of the past two years.[1] From here, I watch the Walpole Island First Nation ferry follow its half-moon shaped route to the American town in which I am standing.[2] I notice that the window that the ferry driver looks out of is darkened, making it impossible to see her/his face. This reminds me of the tinted windows on some of the residents' cars, a fact made complex by the mixture of pride, defiance, and shame it represents. The ferry docks briefly, allowing cars and a few foot passengers to disembark. All reserve residents, each driver and every passenger, will invariably return to Walpole Island carrying such items as cheap cigarettes and candy bars. These items represent the changes in the material lives of the reserve residents as well as the outside ideas that are eroding some of what makes this place unique. I think about how this process of erosion works, likening it to the way that each puff of a Marlboro cigarette sticks to a windshield, giving off the unmistakable odour of American tobacco. If you are a smoker, you tend not to notice it much; but it is there, and it is palpable and strong.

I was waiting for the ferry that was to return me from Bowling Green, Ohio, where I was teaching part-time as a doctoral candidate, to my home on Walpole Island. This was the second of my

---

1. I make use of the first person pronoun in the introductory section of Chapter 1 in order to locate myself in the text and to provide some indication to the audience of how and why this book came about. I hope that this brief discussion will help the reader decide whether she or he will find this book of interest.
2. I refer to Walpole Island as a place, a people, and a reserve.

two stays in the community, and, on this particular night, I was late (if there can be such a thing as being late on Walpole Island) for a meeting with the cultural committee—a meeting at which I was to update my progress on my dissertation. I was in a melancholy mood, having just received a rejection letter from a university in Vancouver, British Columbia, where I was hoping to do some part-time teaching. I clearly remember watching the ferry make its way, wishing I had done my dissertation, indeed, my whole Ph.D. program, differently. I wished I had been more pragmatic, more circumscribed, and less malleable. Why had I come here anyway?

I vaguely recalled my interest in theorizing about the prevalence of "bumper sticker boosterism" as a contemporary form of social movement participation. I was trying to understand the romantic pull of the 1960s for my generation—the post-boomers—and the seeming preference for protests over paychecks that marked that era. This led to my reading about groups that contradicted my hypothesis about my generation which, unlike that of the 1960s, only engages in social activism through the use of bumper stickers and tax deductible donations. These groups were made up of grassroots activists who were part of the environmental justice movement. I discovered that these community-based groups were comprised of people who invested tremendous amounts of their time and energy to ensuring that their families and communities were safe from the harm caused by environmental degradation. The environmental justice movement focuses attention on the effects of pollution among both urban and rural working people. Many of the local and national leaders of the environmental justice movement are women and people of color. These leaders have put forward a politics of empowerment that has challenged the traditional separation of work and community and raised fundamental issues about how the economy hurts certain communities—hurts them in ways that conflict with alleged values concerning equal protection under the law and a "fair playing field." Finally, the environmental justice movement has challenged the large, mainstream environmental groups that have grown distant from the concerns and living conditions of average North Americans.

Especially captivating to me were the scientific and popular accounts of Walpole Island's fight to ensure that the surreal blue waters of the St. Clair River, which surround the community, would not continue to bear toxins. These toxins, found in fish, ducks, and various animals that call Walpole Island home, emanate from fifty-two industrial sources (including thermo-electric generating stations, petroleum refineries, organic and inorganic chemical manufacturers, paper companies, salt producers, and municipal wastewater treatment plants). The list of prominent and powerful companies involved include Esso, Shell, Dow, Sun Oil, Dome, Novocar, and Chinook. From 1986 to 1992, these offenders produced 550 chemical spills, seventeen of which were severe enough to force Walpole Island's water treatment plant to shut down. Walpole Island was being polluted because the First Nation living there did not have the power to stop companies from discharging their waste into the St. Clair River and calling it a spill. Discharges and spills are a normal part of doing business. If these discharges/spills haven't already done so, it is only a matter of time before they seriously harm the health of residents.

Walpole's environmental justice plight intensified my theoretical interest in grassroots activism. It led me to recognize the huge and underacknowledged difference between signing a check and engaging in collective action. Walpole Island is a First Nation with a long history of wresting cultural autonomy from oppressive forces. This oppression has often been insidious, frequently appearing as benevolent paternalism, and it has resulted in a contemporary struggle to find the confidence and resources to create strategies to fight for an identifiable and personally meaningful Walpole Island culture. I quickly became immersed in this world.

WALPOLE ISLAND: RECENT HISTORY

As a result of assimilationist goals epitomized by the reserve system, the late nineteenth century saw the development of small-scale farming on Walpole Island. In addition, this era saw the implementation of the Indian Act, 1876.[3] This act prevented the outright ownership and sale of land on the reserve and, paradoxically, led to the government's policy of promoting individualized

---

3. The Indian Act, 1876, completely abolished any form of self-government for Native peoples. It also introduced the "location ticket system," which permitted specific individuals to own specific parcels of land on the reserve. The act ensured that ownership of the land would remain with the family first and, ultimately, with the band. The location ticket system eventually led to an unequal distribution of income and wealth among community members.

property through the issuing of ownership tickets (Francis 1992). Again, this was done to introduce Native cultures to the concept of private property and was part of the larger project of assimilation. As Francis (1992, 203) explains: "The fact that Native people seemed to lack a sense of private ownership was widely regarded as a sign of their backwardness. Tribalism, or tribal communism as some people called it, was blamed for stifling the development of initiative and personal responsibility." The impact of the Indian Act was primarily social, with a shift from "communal organization of production and the concomitant egalitarian ethic of sharing" to "social differentiation" in the form of small, family plots (VanWyck 1992, 234).

The decision to implement the Indian Act and the location ticket system were catalysts for a major community issue—one that still hampers the establishment of a core collective identity; that is, the contentious issue of band membership and Native status. As Frideres (1993, 28) explains, there are three major Native subgroups: legal, registered, or status; non-status; and Métis. Legal, or status, Natives have federal legal status, meaning that they are under the administrative influence of the federal government (Frideres 1993, 30). Achieving band status today generally means being attached to a band that is acknowledged to exist by the federal government. Most status Natives belong to bands, which have rights to reserve lands held in common. Bands are a legal/political construction of the federal government. Used largely for administrative purposes, bands group together Native peoples based on perceived common interests in land and money (Frideres 1993, 145).

The example of the chief who was in power during my stay is instructive. He was an evangelist and is currently a lay priest in the evangelical church. He has upset the community (particularly those who dislike his religious affiliation), and there have been many complaints about his politics. He was blamed for the failure of Walpole Island First Nation residents to get jobs in the construction of a day-care center as well as for the negotiation of a new policing agreement that gave the Royal Canadian Mounted Police the right to come on the reserve, thereby weakening community self-policing and self-determination. This person's band membership was gained as a product of an amendment (Bill C-31) to the Indian Act. Since his mother, but not his father, is from Walpole Island, before Bill C-31 he would not have been eligible for band membership. Hostile signs and hand-drawn pamphlets depicted him as, at various points, Judas Iscariot and the devil. One particularly telling sign made reference to the chief's C-31 status and his status as an apple (red on the outside, white on the inside). The beginning of the twentieth century was the beginning of a forty-year transition to off-reserve wage labor for those on Walpole Island. Agricultural land was leased to off-reserve farmers and work was sought in nearby Algonac (Michigan) or Wallaceburg (Ontario). The shift from the family farm to the factory meant that the opportunity for assimilationist efforts to play themselves out according to the Indian Act, 1876, were lost. However, as the above example shows, assimilationist goals were and are being realized through the continued importance of band membership and its repercussions for community solidarity. The reserve system removed the possibility of using one's land as collateral and destroyed the possibility of receiving operating loans for growing crops.

The depression of the 1930s brought the farm-to-factory transformation to a near halt, but momentum was intensified with the economic boom brought about by the World War II. Indeed, wage labor as a source of income was all the more pronounced for the Walpole Island population because, as mentioned, the Indian Act, 1876, made it impossible to use the land as collateral to get a loan (NIN.DA.WAAB.JIG 1987).[4] This meant that economic participation, in an increasingly rationalized and capital-intensive environment, was impossible for Walpole Island residents. Large-scale farming was out of the question, and it was necessary for both men and women to sell their labor off-reserve, thus further "undermin[ing] farming on a family household basis, and therefore the forms of household and community that had been created" (VanWyck 1992, 306).

Accordingly, the 1950s and 1960s were periods of declining interest in reserve farming. Indeed, at one point, only one farm was operated by Walpole Island residents, and the remaining land was leased out to non-Native farmers. The leasing of land to outside entrepreneurs occurred for two major reasons. First, it was the result of a postwar economy that consisted of increased job competition and vulnerability to outside economic forces. Second, and more important, the Walpole Island community had lost

---

4. If reserve land could have been sold, in all likelihood there would not be a Walpole Island community today.

control over its own resources, which were subject to the whims of the Department of Indian Affairs and its agent. In general, the result was increasing unemployment and government dependency: situations that exaggerated the painful repercussions of the move from community to individual self-sufficiency. Jacobs (1990, 27) describes this process:

> All land title on a reserve is vested in Her Majesty's name, and the Indian agent, being an agent of the crown, was the only person authorized to sign contracts that were in any way associated with the reserve. And as all business directly or indirectly dealt with reserve land, this meant that the agent had his hand in practically everything—the management of roads, bridges, schools, housing, welfare, leasing of land, sale of timber, policing, and many others.

Exacerbating almost all the aforementioned forces of dependence and negligence was the advent of the residential school experience. Residential schools are an extremely sensitive topic among Native people, and the subject came up several times in discussions about the sources of unhealthy elements in the community.[5] As an elder named Joseph explains:

> Some of those social ills in the community have been caused by the residential school holocaust that went on. It stripped a lot of the Native people of their dignity, confidence, self-esteem, and pride that I think we always had as a people. It is only now that we are starting to heal ourselves of those injustices that were done, and I think that will take a few generations.

Compulsory attendance at residential schools meant that children and adolescents were away from their homes for extended periods of time. Residential schools were operated by different church denominations, but they were funded by the federal government. They were, in fact, the federal government's attempt to assimilate Native youth. Children were punished for speaking their language or otherwise expressing their culture. The impact

---

5. I am not attempting to make a general assessment of the residential school experience for Walpole residents. The discussion that follows is included because residents talked about the schools during our conversations pertaining to the subject matter of this book.

of these schools on Walpole Island's history is generally negative, and its effects are still considerable. As Joseph recalls:

Years ago, when I went to school I used to get a whoppin' if I spoke our language. Now they don't send kids to boarding school anymore. I did not have to go to boarding school, but I had too far to walk and the snow bank was taller than I was and I wasn't capable, so I put in my application to go away and away I went. I didn't want to leave here, but I had to go to school or they would have took me out anyway; if I didn't go, they'd have put me where they wanted to put me.

The most devastating consequence of residential schools was the destruction of Native ways of knowing. For example, clan memberships and Native names—critical ancestral links determining lines of descent—were forgotten. One interviewee estimated that, today, only 10 percent of the community know their clan affiliation.

As the 1960s unfolded, it was the practice of leasing land out to non-Native farmers that provided the fodder for those in the Walpole Island community who advocated self-government. Specifically, the Indian agent's control over the leasing of agricultural land and the subsequent lack of community autonomy was an increasing cause of frustration. Accordingly, the residents sought administrative independence by attempting to have the Indian agent removed from Walpole Island—the first attempt of its kind in Canada (Jacobs 1990; NIN.DA.WAAB.JIG 1987). A new leadership emerged on Walpole Island and eventually "negotiated the removal of the Indian Agent and the terms of what they referred to as 'self-government'" (VanWyck 1992, 361). This brought new possibilities for Walpole Islanders, who implemented new plans and projects to usher in the present era (Jacobs 1990).[6]

---

6. The band council was under a great deal of pressure during my time on Walpole Island. The following comment is sympathetic toward the council:

We have jobs to go to every day and families to feed and that, we elect people and put people in positions to do that for us, they're supposed to represent us. When they're trying to represent us, different groups are constantly knocking them down, making their jobs ten times harder. I also thought whenever you got a chief and council they were going to represent you for two years. If you had a concern you went to the chief and council and discussed it with them.

Under this regime, Native populations were encouraged to move to Walpole Island and to become farmers, with little regard for either the cultural predispositions of the people or the suitability of the land for agriculture. Today, farming represents a viable commercial enterprise, given the presence of substantial portions of wetlands and marsh. The major project symbolizing the Walpole Island community's pursuit of economic and cultural autonomy is the band-owned and -operated agricultural cooperative. Tahgahoning Enterprise is the commercial effort that embeds the community within the larger socio-economic logic of capitalism. Yet it also represents the struggle of the population to come to terms with those historical forces, both political and social, that were decimating the community. In showing that an economically viable commercial enterprise could be undertaken profitably, possibilities for employment and income were created and kept in balance with community values. This agricultural cooperative today oversees the production of 4,500 acres, with prospects for additional growth looking very positive.

The community of Walpole Island is poised on the Canada/United States boundary at the very edge of the Canadian border. This location is of larger significance when one remembers that the community's territory is unceded; that is, that it is a reserve of land left to Native people but never accorded private property rights. Walpole Island has had to struggle to maintain itself as a distinct culture, not only in the past, but also in the face of current attempts to use this community as the kidney of the Great Lakes. A variety of social and historical forces have structured a community whose ability to supply itself with an autonomous set of meanings is a testament to the resiliency of its people. While early residents fought to maintain political autonomy in the face of efforts to assimilate them, the contemporary community battles multinational forces that wish to use it as a sewage system.

I want to look at how a core set of culturally embedded meanings—those that underscore the ecological Native/sustainable community collective action frame—have endowed the Walpole community with counter-hegemonic potential. This potential may be seen with regard to environmental issues, as Walpole Islanders embody the mainstream dream of/desire for harmonious relations between the human and the non-human worlds.

WALPOLE ISLAND TODAY

The Walpole Island First Nations reserve (#46), or Bkejwanong ("the place where water divides"), in Ontario is the southernmost reserve in Canada. Walpole consists of 2,300 permanent residents from a band membership of 3,100. This official count does not acknowledge the fact that the population size is extremely fluid because of short-term moves off of and onto the reserve. Walpole Island is still almost entirely populated by people from the Ottawa, Ojibway, and Potawatomi Nations.

Sources of identity and pride dictate the retention of traditional economic and cultural practices despite the proximity of large, non-Native urban centers such as Detroit and Windsor. The obvious impact of these large urban centers notwithstanding, Walpole Island still has residents who can speak the local dialect and weave baskets out of black ash. The approximately ninety-one square kilometers that compose this community are situated in the extreme northeastern corner of the mouth of the St. Clair River. The land mass is shaped like a bird's foot, and it circumscribes the Canadian portion of the Lake St. Clair wetland delta. It is surrounded by water on all three sides: the St. Clair River on the northwest; Le Chenail Ecarte, or Snye River, on the northeast; and Lake St. Clair on the south. These waters and their tributaries are primarily responsible for having fashioned nine separate islands: six Canadian (St. Anne, Walpole, Squirrel, Potawatomi, Bassett, and Seaway) and three American (Harsens, Russell, and Dickinson).

The St. Clair River was formed when a strait connecting prehistoric Lake Huron and Lake Erie was filled with retreating glacial waters. This strait carried sediment from the shorelines of the upper Great Lakes and deposited it at the mouth of the river forming the delta that is now home to Walpole Island. Walpole Island is a digitate, or bird-foot, delta, containing long extensions that branch out into the open water of Lake St. Clair. This type of delta features lake bottom that gently slopes away from the mouth of the river and is conducive to the build-up of natural levees. These levees are the site of what is referred to as a delta wetland.

Residences are concentrated in the northern half of the reserve, which is the highest and driest part of Walpole Island.

Housing is primarily distributed along forty kilometers of road-way on approximately thirty-one square kilometers of land. With the exception of the wetland areas, homes are haphazardly lo-cated all over the community. Officially there are 345 houses, thirty-seven of which are found in one of only two subdivisions on the island. A significantly larger number of water bills are dis-tributed however, suggesting the existence of many more homes. The houses are generally small, with lots of space between them, and they are built according to a variety of styles. While there are some older-style log homes (with mortar connecting rough-hewn logs) and some expensive brick ranch-style dwellings, most newer homes are modest aluminum-sided affairs, each of which contains about 1,200 square feet of living space. While concern over lawns and lawn ornaments is not widespread on Walpole Is-land, many lawns are carefully manicured and adorned. A few homes reflect the stereotype of the reserve, with abandoned cars being their major adornment. Housing has broad social implica-tions within the community. Homes deemed ostentatious are seen as giving evidence of their occupants wishing to copy the White homes across the St. Clair or Snye Rivers. More rarely, these os-tentatious homes are perceived to be evidence of preferential treatment by the local government (i.e., the band council).

There are a large number of administrative and government program offices, and these are in fairly close proximity to each other. Along a brief stretch of road heading south and then east from the Algonac ferry there are the Walpole Island Council building, the fire department, the health center, the seniors com-plex, the day nursery, the elementary school, and Tahgahoning Enterprises (a Walpole Island agriculture cooperative that main-tains 4,000+ acres). The island lacks a traditional downtown area, but it does have a variety store, a ferry landing, and many homes and cottages. These buildings constitute the "heart of Walpole Is-land," a fact that is underscored in the summer, when vacationers and tourists augment the regulars. Recently, however, the first strip mall on the island has just been built. Somewhat inexplica-bly, it is situated near the eastern edge of the island, near the com-munity center, rather than near the ferry landing. The community center features a popular and noisy local restaurant named the Penalty Box. The Penalty Box adjoins two other popular loca-tions, the local ice arena and the community center proper, which is the site of public meetings, banquets, and other events.

Because they are also part of the delta, the relatively densely populated American communities of Algonac, Harsens, and Russel are located directly across the St. Clair River from Walpole Island. The river width varies between these communities and Walpole, but it is never great enough to prevent the detection of difference. These three non-Native vacation communities feature many large, stately homes and huge boats. The area's wealth is the combined product of its having economic roots in wartime industry and being a popular vacation area. The resulting affluence has meant that many Walpole Island residents have been able to get employment as factory workers or domestic servants. Today these American locations, as well as others further up the St. Clair River on the American side, are favorite spots for both residents of, and vacationers to, Walpole Island. In particular, items such as beer, restaurant food, and groceries are considerably cheaper on the American than the Canadian side of the river. Walpole Island vacationers seem to take particular delight in filling up their boats with cheap American gas at the various marinas located "across the river"; Walpole residents are used to it. It is not surprising to see small water craft leave Walpole, cross over to Algonac, and return after just a few minutes. Immigration authorities pay little attention to these less than clandestine activities, perhaps respecting Native beliefs regarding the right of free passage or, more likely, reflecting the unlikelihood of being able to monitor such activity. The degree of cross-border activity is also partially suggested by the lack of marinas and restaurants on Walpole Island.

One of the telltale experiences that stands out in my mind as a reflection of the contradictions of this place revolves around the annual fourth of July fair fireworks hosted by Algonac. This event is heavily attended by members of the Walpole Island community, who gather on the Walpole Island beach-front area directly across from Algonac to watch the fireworks. Great cheers erupt on the beach following particularly well-staged explosions. It struck me that there was something quite ironic about the fact that I was watching the residents of a First Nation celebrating American nationhood—a country whose emergence came at the expense of the ancestors of those from whom I was hearing laughter and clapping.

Fireworks season soon gives way to fall, and the winter resident is treated to the serenity that accompanies even the thinnest blanket of snow, which muffles the infrequent sounds of cars going in and out of driveways or to the community center. One element of the winter landscape that captivated me was the ice jams created by the flow of ice from Lake Huron into the narrow St. Clair River. Vast expanses of drift ice pile into other floes, creating an uneven and somewhat surreal picture as one journeys along the St. Clair River in late winter. Indeed, watching the persistent efforts of the ice-breakers and listening to the sounds of the battle between ice and boat is one clear indication that spring is coming.

When the weather warms, there is an outbreak of activity. People emerge in inverse proportion to the fading winter season. As there are few sidewalks in the community, the roads are shared by pedestrians, bikes, vehicles, and dogs, and the rules guiding this traffic are uncertain at best. In addition, the waters are filled with fish and those who hope to catch them. The small aluminum fishing boats favored by Walpole Island residents share space with giant Great Lakes and ocean freighters that transport their cargo along this connecting waterway. Cottages that are owned by vacationers are opened, and ferries to and from the United States are frequent.

During my first extended visit to Walpole Island I had to leave the community once a week in order to teach. Upon returning, usually the following day, I always felt relieved when I was the recipient of a brief nod or wave. Despite my transitory presence, I was forming an attachment to Walpole Island that made the fight to save it from environmental degradation all the more compelling for me. Another contributing factor to my attachment to the community was the way that the chemical spills called the community members to action and crystallized how they felt about environmental degradation. The consciousness underscoring this collective action alerted me to how my research on Walpole Island could be linked to other examples of grassroots activism. It occurred to me that, through the notion of social movements, I could conceptualize the interplay between culture and ideology.

FRAMING THE DEBATE: COLLECTIVE ACTION AND IDENTITY

Social movements are a form of local, collective advocacy that promotes changes in power relations. Social movements always develop in a particular period and so reflect a particular historical and cultural context. Organizers hope to gain committed members by relating their causes to existing social conditions. In other words, whether or not community members will "try on" the movement has much to do with the ability of organizers to represent—in their ideas and strategies—issues and meanings that have relevance to the community.

Today, the excitement of social movement scholarship comes from research and writings that analyze the issues of culture, ideology, and framing. This literature comes from the disciplines of political science, sociology, social psychology, and anthropology. Contributions have created a variety of new methodologies, theories, and conceptual approaches that often use examples from community activism in order to bring social movements down to the local scale and to enhance our understanding of them. The result of this is that community-based research is in vogue.

The relatively small populations involved in community-level collective protest have resulted in social movement literature addressing the significant role that meaning has for the individual. According to Rogers (1998, 78), human consciousness combined with intentionality constitute meanings via the making and sharing of reality. This rendering of meaning draws upon Husserl's (1970, 285) notion of a local lifeworld, "a communal system of meanings" that influences one's understanding of all experience. Knowledge, then, is produced through shared meanings rather than a priori categories. The process of attaching meaning involves interaction and, therefore, the groups we belong to—be they family or community—are sources of meanings.[7] Meanings then, are the product of "perceptions, moods, cognitions, beliefs and the symbols, images, texts, rituals, conversations through which...inner ideas and sentiments are communicated" (Oberschall 1993, 188). The issue of meaning has renewed interest in

---

7. Attaching meaning involves the process of tying motives to the objective(s) that drive action. My favorite way of thinking about this involves Don McLean's famous song "American Pie." The real attraction of this song is its historical references, such as "the day the music died" (i.e., the day Buddy Holly died). McLean had been constantly asked what the song meant to him. One day he answered: "it means that I never have had to work a day in my life." If it is assumed that McLean wanted this song to take on the status that it has, then we can infer that fame, and presumably fortune, were the motives driving the goal of creating lyrics whose broad historical sweep and subject matter lay at the foundation of this generational anthem.

some of the concepts that appeared in the earlier collective behavior literature.

As the predecessor of social psychological investigations of why people participate in social mobilization, collective behavior research conceptualizes any kind of participation (including that involved in riots and mobs) as an unpredictable social activity. This definition characterizes the early views on social protest activity, which implied that those individuals involved in collective behavior were of marginal social standing and had inherent predispositions for erratic behavior. Early social movement theorists wanted to define their area of interest in opposition to how collective behavior theorists had defined theirs; that is, the former insisted that social movements were predictable phenomena that could be explained by researching their goals, tactics, organizations, and resources. Because of this, neither subjective factors nor cultural conditions were manifestly included in investigations of the root cause of collective action. Not including either of these eliminates uncertainty and implies predictability.

At the same time, it is inaccurate to suggest that social movement theorists have not attempted to answer, often in contradictory ways, questions related to understanding individual reasons for participating in social protest activity. These answers have suggested that such participation has to do with: an irrational response, a rational choice, the structure of political opportunities, a lack of repression, an absence of wider social breakdown, and social networks. More recently, individual participation in collective activity has been seen as the product of patterns of interaction that are seen as intruding into our private lives. For example, the concept of ethnicity is reinforced in our use of language and the patterns of settlement. The point in all of this for us is that mobilization—as a concept describing like-minded individuals who do participate in the movement—expresses the individual's confidence that collective action will acknowledge and potentially solve social injustice.

The problem, as I see it, is that social movement theorists have been intent upon escaping being lumped together with collective behaviorists. This studied avoidance of the individual has meant that the social construction of reality, and its focus on social interaction—the "why" of social movement participation—has been made peripheral to the seemingly more significant issue of "how" such mobilization occurs.

The two dominant developments that social movement theorists have pursued, following the collective behaviorists, took radically different paths towards explaining how organizations attempt to mobilize an individual's time, money, and energy. The resource mobilization (RM) tradition argues that social movement formations are based upon whatever resources and opportunities support the appropriate collective action. This model of social movements focuses on organizational forms, modes of communication, the rational individual, and the political environment. Accordingly, the mobilization of the rational individual is determined by a cost-benefit analysis of the collective activity in question, so the likelihood of the movement's success and/or the incentives it offers are seen as overarching determinants of individual participation. The RM tradition's explanatory power can be seen with regard to the environmental justice movement, wherein individual social movement organizations (SMOs) have drawn heavily upon the membership of large national or international environmental organizations (despite a general ambivalence toward mainstream environmental groups). According to the RM tradition, it is logical that individual groups would seek to exploit the resources of larger bodies while experiencing the more immediate and intimate rewards available in small collections of activists.

The second path, the new social movement (NSM) tradition, is preoccupied with the emergence of a set of new values and activities that undergird the formation of a constituency. A constituency refers to all the like-minded individuals who could potentially participate in the movement. But "new" theorists are usually suggesting social movements that are not originating from one's class position and the social relations that result. Theorists sympathetic to the NSM model assert that society is a terrain for struggles over the recognition of new societal norms, which are connected to values. It follows that individual mobilization is a response to (1) collective beliefs about what is right and (2) the possibilities of constructing a group identity around whatever it is that has been so defined. For example, the SMOs that compose the environmental justice movement work alone or with regional networks rather than with large environmental organizations. This decision to remain local reflects the values of the membership, which privilege small grassroots non-professional efforts to change power arrangements. The NSM model would explain these SMOs by arguing that they recruit individuals who recognize the importance of such values.

Although quite different, both the RM and the NSM models tend to treat the individual in a simplistic fashion in that they both take her/his participation as a foregone conclusion once certain socio-structural/psychological factors are satisfied. In short, both RM and NSM models are unable to adequately account for the individual in terms of cultural, historical, and experiential factors.

In my view, the shortcoming of both explanations is their reliance on an ahistorical understanding of community-based work. With regard to the Heritage Centre, for example, it must be understood as a political component of the community's Native identity, one that needs a macro-sociological perspective to be explained. One needs to scrutinize the push and pull of historical relations between Native and non-Native populations in Canada, especially against the relatively recent and quite radical decisions by Walpole Island and other First Nations to accept stakeholder status (Frideres 1993, 281–331). Though both historical and contemporary relations are factors, I do not think the environmental justice movement on Walpole Island is merely the serendipitous result of a benevolent Canadian state and a politically astute First Nation. It is the product, like many social activities, of untold interactions and the meanings these facilitate.

Social movement scholars have begun to reconcile the aforementioned gaps by bringing together the RM focus on material conditions/resources and the NSM focus on collective identity and discourse. Although loosely conceptualized (Zald 1996) and only recently addressed (cf. Johnston and Klandermans 1995; Klandermans 1992; Larana et al. 1994; Klandermans et al. 1988; Morris and McClurg-Mueller 1992), this reconciliation—called the synthesis perspective—combines two views of how meaning is attached to objects and actions. And it is this perspective that I use in my analysis.

The synthesis perspective enables social movement theorists to better explore the cultural resources that play a part in individual mobilization. In so doing, the synthesis model provides the grounds for concentrating on the construction of subjective meanings—the beliefs and values that are the product of the individual's cultural context. In other words, these scholars favor a dynamic conception of culture, with individuals being viewed as ordering, interpreting, and resisting various systems of ideas. And this dynamic conception of culture means accepting the fact that reality, as such, is socially constructed. And this "reality" is constantly undergoing a process of cognitive filtering, which often results in an ideology—a set of values that is derived from societal notions of what is significant and meaningful and that often guides our behavior.[8] Of course, the values and beliefs that permeate human interaction are all elements of culture. These values and beliefs are negotiated by the individual, who uses images and ideas to formulate a personal response to existing conditions. Culture is a set of commonsense practices that both reflect and shape a socially constructed "reality." This definition assumes two things: first, that commonsense practices are narrowly defined by social institutions and, second, that all social phenomena are the product of social activity. This recognition that culture is extracted from social practices and then translated into collective action supports Marx Feree's (1992, 41) claim that "all values, including those that appear to be 'natural' and 'objective,' rest in social experience of some sort" and create "historically embodied, concrete persons." In other words, reality is a social construct.

The social construction of reality is at the heart of a phenomenological approach to meaning—an approach that examines the process by which the everyday reality of social actors is constructed, ordered, and then taken for granted. This leads to an examination of the formulation of subjective meanings, which, in turn, illuminates two processes that are integral to social movement participation: (1) the way that everyday practices result in versions of reality and (2) the way that challenges to these practices become sites for struggle. A similar explanation is put forward by Bash (1995, 9), who defines subjective meanings as being

> guided by the collectively negotiated conceptions, ordering principles, and valuations that are conditioned by a people's history and that arise in their social life. They resonate with a particular society's culture; they constitute its

---

8. Of course, ideologies often contain their own contradictions. For example, even though Canada has an international reputation for compassion, its value system underscores the desire for a very high standard of living and thus supports actions that limit global equality. The result: we don't feel morally compelled to improve the lot of the dispossessed, impoverished, or oppressed because that would involve recognizing massive contradictions between being compassionate and condoning actions that directly reinforce global inequality.

taken-for-granteds; they permeate its dominant ideology; and they legitimate what is considered as conventional wisdom.

These theoretical points inform the concrete steps that the Walpole Island First Nation has formally taken in confronting the chemical spills that threaten the sustainability of this community. At the formal level of movement activity, the Heritage Centre (Nin.da.waab.jig) is at the forefront. However, there is also an informal level of movement activity that steadily infuses the community's laudable efforts at resistance. I argue that this informal level of movement activity is leveraged by what Francis (1992) refers to as the notion of the "ecological Native." The ecological Native is a socially constructed identity that posits First Nations peoples as role models for how to achieve sustainability. This "green" Aboriginal identity has great potency because it: (1) partially assuages White guilt over pollution and (2) points to some uncomfortable knowledge concerning the quest for a Canadian identity.

The Canadian identity—and at some level every Canadian citizen knows this—has been heretofore forged out of a farcical history of English and French exploration and settlement—a history that barely acknowledges the cost in Aboriginal lives and cultures. This national imaginary mocks the colonization and subjugation of Aboriginal peoples. We are only now painfully turning to the colonized themselves. And the acceptance of the ecological Native stereotype is popular because it seems to enable a mainstream recognition of an authentic Aboriginal contribution to the Canadian identity. Being Canadian has been heavily infused with being Native. Proof of this may be found in Valda Blundell's (1993) discussion of the stereotypical depiction of Native populations prominent in tourist areas. The assorted "Native" crafts that are so popular with tourists constitute much of what the outside world identifies as Canadian.

Consider, for example, the 1997 adoption of a new logo by the National Hockey League's Vancouver Canucks. This logo, featuring a highly stylized killer whale leaping out of the ocean, clearly ties a corporation (Orca Bay) to indigenous populations of the Northwest Coast. Orca Bay's use of this blue, purple, orange, and white killer whale to represent a team named the Canucks recalls both bona fide indigenous cultural forms and their commodification by fur traders, government officials, and anthropologists. Johnny Canuck as a cultural icon is nested in a Native signifier. Interestingly, the decision to introduce this symbol led to a perceived rise in the number of Native souvenirs being sold in Gastown and other tourist enclaves in Vancouver that either featured the killer whale or the color combination chosen by Orca Bay for the Canucks' jerseys. Assuming that a few of these items are manufactured by Native people, and this is an assumption, it is safe to say that some Native peoples' economic circumstances were improved by Orca Bay's merchandising of its hockey team. In other words, Native peoples may be purposefully rearticulating the meanings connected to their continued exploitation in ways that reaffirm sympathetic mainstream sentiment and foster collective identity not only to sell tourist souvenirs, but also to invigorate Native consciousness.

I want to examine the Walpole Island "ecological Native" as a stereotype that is important to making the community aware of the possibilities of radically reconceptualizing its identity through making a self-conscious break with a subjugated past. Any community engaged in such work can be conceived of as part of the environmental justice movement, albeit a new force within that movement—one that draws upon images of Native people as the shepherds of the planet, thus coalescing mainstream symbolic markers of Nativeness in order to mobilize sympathy for the cause. This offers an opportunity to promote new meanings concerning how Aboriginal peoples ought to be seen within contemporary Canada.

Based on my experiences, the green community identity appeals to the Walpole Island community's belief that there is a distinct lack of mainstream compassion for its environmental concerns. I also believe that sustainability fits with community members seeing their lives as congruent with what Trigger (1996, 65) refers to as "genuine traditional aboriginal notions regarding appropriate human relations with land and natural resources." Examples of such sentiment include the Anishinabe seventh generation prophecy (see Chapter 3), which foretells the coming ascendance of Native status and predicts that Native populations will become role models because of a universal reawakening to the notion that communities with an extensive history of interacting with a particular terrain (what Nabhan refers to as "cultures of habitat") are the key to sustaining the environment. In light of powerful outside forces that threaten the health of the Walpole Island community, the Heritage Centre attempts to mobilize people through referring to their cultural heritage and their status as once and future protectors of the environment.

Underlying all of the Heritage Centre's efforts then, is the desire to recruit community members through referring to toxic discharges in terms of injustice, identity, Nativeness, and sustainability. In the language of social movement theory, what I am concerned with is the cultivation of ideological links between the Heritage Centre and a pool of potential constituents. The concepts of "frame," "collective action frames," and "frame alignment" are useful with regard to showing that social movement and grassroots organizations like the Heritage Centre are signifying agents actively involved in the contextualization of events and conditions and, thus, are active in responding to, and in producing, meanings for potential adherents/constituents.

"Frame" refers to the cognitive plan that individuals employ to simplify and condense the "world out there" by selectively applying lesser or greater significance to issues, events, experiences, and actions. By paying attention to frames it is possible to assess the potency of collective action. "Collective action frames" are meaning packages that organizers use to call attention to the roots of, and common solutions to, a perceived injustice. The goal is to inspire and legitimate collective activity. "Frame alignment" highlights the fitting together of frame and collective action frame in the mobilization of adherents/constituents. In other words, frame alignment describes "the efforts by which organizers seek to join the cognitive orientations of individuals with the collective action frames of the social movement organizations" (McAdam 1994, 37).

In the case of Walpole Island, frame alignment—the meeting of frame and collective action frame—is negotiated against the backdrop of modernity. Modernity, at its most dangerous, involves a shift in emphasis from the local to the global—in this case global capital. Thus modernity encroaches and ultimately encompasses the local, corrupting identity and producing categories and knowledge that alienate people from one another. Transcending local identity entails overcoming a resident's Husserlian lifeworld—the specifics of place that are largely constitutive of her/his self-image and self-definition. In the case of Walpole Island's search for environmental justice, this means peeling back some layers of the "authentic" Native identity that is buttressing the green movement, looking at the internalization of this identity, and assessing how it has been "staked out" as a weapon against the incursion of the unfettered capital that is responsible for environmental degradation The Heritage Centre's collective action frame may be defined as "ecological Native/sustainable community." Having a sustainable community involves working toward equitable social, economic, cultural, and technological betterment in a way that does not pollute ecosystems and irrevocably deplete natural resources. Sustainability involves cleaning up past pollution and ensuring that chemicals, agricultural pesticides, and other contaminants do not destroy more species or damage the health of humans and wildlife. Sustainability often involves reintroducing some plants and animals that have disappeared from an area and putting an end to further wetland loss. Sustainability does not mean an end to development.

As a representative of the Walpole Island community, the Heritage Centre is aware of what is involved in attaching meaning to the concept of sustainable development. While this is, by and large, an integrative process with important possibilities for fostering solidarity, it does have to overcome a number of internal divisions. These divisions will be discussed in greater detail later, but for now let me just say, following Hornborg (1994), that they are based on band politics (who voted for whom in the last election), religion (traditional versus Christian), family (to whom is one related), and funding (who is eligible for local, provincial, and/or federal programs).

THE TRUTH ABOUT THE QUESTIONS

It is important to understand that the residents of Walpole Island do not conceive of environmental protection activities in terms of social movement participation or abstract discussions of framing activities. However, I use such analytical terms because they provide a strong theoretical foundation for showing how this community can teach other communities about the process of becoming politically organized. My position vis-à-vis Walpole Island is that of a researcher interpreting theory in a context that has enormous potential for illustrating the role of personal beliefs within a collective action frame.

With regard to Walpole Island, I hope to show the importance of collective identity to the protection of the natural resources and the survival of community practices, beliefs, and values. In doing this I focus on the Heritage Centre's ability to engage local meanings in support of collective activity. My contention is that Walpole Island's concerns fit nicely within an emerging environmental justice frame. This claim will be tested by looking at the indigenous cultural identifiers that the Walpole Island community articulates in its response to the Heritage Centre.

I take for granted that reality is socially constructed and that it is adapted, framed, and reformulated by the individual. Given this, I ask how individuals are mobilized into participating in social movements. I look at Walpole Island's environmental protection efforts (and its location within a broader environmental justice movement), and I show how meanings are embedded in the particularities of culture.

COMING ATTRACTIONS

In Chapter 2 I discuss the Heritage Centre and its values. In Chapters 3, 4, 5, and 6 I discuss, respectively, four critical events in the Heritage Centre's efforts to protect the environment: (1) the existence of a massive toxic blob; (2) the question of whether fresh water should be supplied by a pipeline or a tower; (3) doubts concerning the ability of outside organizations to effectively contribute to the management of the island's marsh; and (4) renewed fears of a whole new round of discharges as a consequence of massive releases of waste water into the St. Clair River. In Chapter 7, I discuss the methodological implications of my findings and make recommendations.

Before going on, however, I would like to briefly address the four critical events around which the middle chapters of this book revolve. These events are defined as critical because they highlight culturally meaningful "facts" concerning the physical, spiritual, and emotional toll of environmental degradation and because they promote collective action. These events are used to examine the struggles over the ideological content of the Heritage Centre's collective action frame (i.e., ecological Native/sustainable community) as it was developed and defined during twenty years of fighting to protect the environment. In other words, I suggest that the struggles over what sustainability meant took place as a series of dialogues concerning Heritage Centre actions and community reactions. Consequently, these four critical events are used to accomplish three tasks: (1) to judge the fit between the Heritage Centre's "ecological Native/sustainable community" collective action frame and those subjective meanings held by the community; (2) to uncover the source of these meanings as they elaborate the collective action frame; and (3) to examine the development and transformation of the collective action frame. The examination of these four events will show how the Heritage Centre's framing efforts acted as a historical nodal point—a time and place in which meaning eventually becomes crystallized.

In elaborating 1996–1998 as a historical nodal point, the process of meaning construction will be made visible against the backdrop of local meanings, values, and beliefs. This examination of the dialogue over frames will highlight the mechanisms involved in meaning construction, specifically emphasizing the fact that frames are cultural representations. This organizing schema can be imagined in terms of layers: the Heritage Centre exists within the Walpole Island community, which, in turn, exists within its natural environment.

The first layer, the Heritage Centre, is described in the next chapter. The second layer is the community of Walpole Island. The residents of Walpole Island accept the burden of reflecting on the environmental repercussions of their activities and accept the responsibility that comes with this. The community of Walpole Island has long been engaged in tempering the impact of uninvited and unwanted outside influences. The result of this self-conscious resistance—the clear rejection of the popular separation of nature and culture, for example—instantiates the potential for mobilizing the community around the environmental justice movement. Examining this process provides a way of looking at the alternately malleable and immutable character of culture.

The third layer is non-human. Walpole Island has a relatively southern climate and is located next to the St. Clair River and Lake St. Clair. Its ecosystem is known as the broadleaf Carolinian life zone. It is renowned for its distinct and rare plants, as exemplified in the tall grass prairie and oak savanna sites. In addition, the St. Clair delta wetland (an undrained marsh) has an extensive growth of plants that remains relatively untouched, despite the fact that the counties that surround Walpole Island have had more than 90 percent of their wetlands converted to other uses. A diverse range of plants, trees, mammals, reptiles, and amphibians is located throughout this habitat, as it provides critical nesting and feeding grounds. Major game fish species include pickerel (also known as walleye or northern pike), yellow perch, and small-mouthed bass. Moreover, 145 bird species have been recorded on Walpole. Popular waterfowl common to Walpole Island include Canada geese, mallards, great blue herons, and red-tailed hawks. In addition, muskrats, raccoons, and approximately twenty other mammal species (including the rare southern flying squirrel) occupy the wetlands.

2

Resources, Values, and the Heritage Centre

One of the clearest signs of the increasingly prominent role of social movements can be seen in the attention that is being paid to them across the disciplines of political science, sociology, social psychology, and anthropology. Much of this attention is focused on social movement organizations (SMOs), independent bodies that share enough beliefs with other SMOs to constitute a social movement. More precisely, an SMO is an established group that becomes the local center for a broader social movement. Somewhat removed from (but representative of) a larger community of potential actors, SMOs combine the talents of individual activists who have a set of skills, contacts, and experience that facilitates the forging of networks and resources. SMOs facilitate favorable conditions for social movements by positively transforming people's attitudes toward the possibility of change. For example, recall that the emergence of the environmental justice movement was the product of small, community-oriented SMOs that fought for safe local environments for work, residence, and play.

HISTORICAL FORCES AND THE BUILDING OF THE HERITAGE CENTRE

At a macrostructural level, it was the reaction of several national Native organizations to the infamous White Paper that provided the impetus for what eventually became the Heritage Centre. The late 1960s and early 1970s witnessed the emergence of a national Native movement. This movement expressed Native frustrations with a marginalized existence—an existence that was the consequence of colonialism in general and the reserve system in particular. A particularly powerful force behind Native political mobilization was the federal Liberal government's 1969 position paper outlining the "unique legal status" of Native people (Miller 1989). The Trudeau government's White Paper called for the end of special status for Native peoples, maintaining that it was this that was responsible for disadvantaging First Nations peoples. The only way to avoid this, so the paper argued, would be to integrate Aboriginal peoples into mainstream Canadian society. This would effectively mean that First Nations peoples would become just another element in multicultural Canada, having neither special rights nor autonomy. The cultural genocide implied by the White Paper generated a great deal of anger within First Nations groups and their sympathizers.

Native outrage created a climate for the revitalization of Aboriginal concerns and led to the organization of a pan-Native movement. Specifically, there was an increase in what Miller (1989, 284) describes as "matters of rhetoric," which involved Aboriginal Canadians making claims of racism and genocide that went largely unheard. More newsworthy was how Aboriginal frustration led to escalating levels of "strategic militancy" within certain elements of the Native movement (Long 1992, 127). Highly visible activities (such as blockades) were used by Native activists to gain media attention and to apply pressure for change. Such actions fostered an ideological terrain that led to new, more outspoken national leadership under the aegis of the National Indian Brotherhood (NIB) (Long 1992, 1996). The NIB was a turning point in Aboriginal political consciousness—"the first national organization run by and for Canada's First Nations" (Long 1996, 381). The NIB saw the White Paper as an attempt at cultural genocide, and it developed the notion of Aboriginal people as "Citizens Plus"—the plus referring to a common Aboriginal spirituality and set of experiences (Long 1992). Long asserts that these experiences are made common by the fact that Aboriginal people had been confined to a particular land base vis-à-vis the reserve system. Ironically, it was the reserve system—designed to control and assimilate Aboriginal people—that provided the grounds for the rise in Native consciousness. One of the Heritage Centre's occasional papers confirms this view, arguing that the emergence of national Native political associations provided the grounds for the community's "recognition of Indian nations" and the "protection of Aboriginal Rights" (Walpole Island Heritage Centre Occasional Paper No. 6 1985, 12).

On Walpole Island, the conflation of political and ideological forces manifested itself in the removal of the Indian agent; the creation of a cultural and community center (home of the arena and the Penalty Box restaurant); a school; a social services center; and, perhaps most critically, a swing bridge that connects the island to the Canadian mainland. It also led to the Walpole Island Band Council's 1973 decision to create a Land Claims Office. The Land Claims Office was a precursor of the Research Group (later renamed the Heritage Centre), which focused on studying and preparing community initiatives regarding the interpretation and implementation of treaties. I asked Dean Jacobs, the current director of the Heritage Centre and former director of both the Land Claims Office and the Research Group, to reflect on the original intent of the Land Claims Office, its relationship to the Research Group, and the values driving national Native politics at that time.

> [The Research Group was organized] to provide up-to-date, accurate information to the community so that they could make good decisions around environmental issues and land claims. We provided that information historically through the Land Claims Office that we started in 1973. As we grew, with the introduction of what was then called the Research Group program, it became more long-term in its objective of building capacity for the community around community-based research in any area that community or chief and council instructed or directed.

Dean's explanation constructs the Research Group as part of a larger cultural reawakening that was fortified by national beliefs in Native autonomy and community control.

The Research Group's work on land claims familiarized the community with, and gave it confidence in, the research process. This was critical to the decision to create a more broad-based effort in the form of the Heritage Centre. A young anthropologist named Sheila VanWyck was a member of the Research Group, and she explains the links between it, the government, and the community's environmental concerns.

> The proposal [to organize the Research Group] had developed originally out of growing public concern about the nature and extent of environmental impact on the reserve from developments such as the St. Lawrence Seaway and the Sarnia petrochemical corridor. Shoreline erosion, mercury contamination, dredging, thermal pollution, industrial air and water pollution, and human

contamination of water resources threatened the natural and human resources of the reserve community. And experience had shown that the reserve could not rely upon the federal government to protect community interests. (VanWyck 1992, 44)

THE HERITAGE CENTRE

Today, the Heritage Centre, which is also known as Nin.da.waab. jig ("those who seek to find"), is located at the north end of Walpole Island in an important spiritual area called Highbanks. It is a large wooden building that overlooks the point where the St. Clair River both continues in a southwesterly direction and channels off to the northeast to become the Snye River. Several Canadian homes and a large marina are situated across the Snye River, while across the St. Clair River is the city of Algonac, Michigan. To the immediate west of the Heritage Centre is a park that has a baseball field, some playground equipment, a big Coast Guard beacon, and some large and stately oak trees.

Inside the Heritage Centre is a disconnected set of rooms that hold combinations of artifacts, memorabilia, and research materials that showcase the community's history, culture, and natural bounty. Tourists, visitors, and schoolchildren often begin their visits to Walpole Island by touring the Heritage Centre, from where they are guided around the rest of the island by one of the staff.

The Heritage Centre's permanent employees usually number four or five. The size of the workforce is hard to measure, as there are a number of employees who move in and out of jobs according to available funding, employment programs, and personal factors. There is no guaranteed annual funding from the band council, although certain employment positions, such as the administrative assistant, are supported on a regular basis. Other funding for employees and research is provided by government programs and by private agencies (which are appealed to on a project-by-project basis). Interim, but often multi-year, funding is available for projects designed to educate students and/or to employ residents. For example, each summer the band and province jointly fund an Environmental Youth Corps program that has young residents clearing trails and assessing the size of the animal population.

The modus operandi of the Heritage Centre blends recruitment with responsibility to the community. Consequently, the Heritage Centre, following adherents of the previously described resource mobilization model, is equal parts command post (McAdam, McCarthy, and Zald 1996) and entrepreneur (McCarthy and Zald 1973). As a command post, the Heritage Centre mediates the attempts of this community to seek changes in corporate practices and to affect government decisions and policies (Zald and Ash 1966). As an entrepreneur, the Heritage Centre uses creative means to represent the grievances of the community, to gather resources, and to accelerate the formation of a social movement (Jenkins 1983).

In order to more fully discern the organizational dynamics of the Heritage Centre, it is useful to look at two internal publications—Walpole Island Heritage Centre Occasional Papers No. 10, 1986, and No. 16, 1989. According to these sources, there are five components to the community-based mandate of the Heritage Centre. The first is to employ residents who, along with experts, engage in a joint effort to conduct community-based research; the second is to ensure the "local control" of research; the third is to establish a reciprocal arrangement between the employees of the Heritage Centre and other residents regarding planning, monitoring, and evaluating programs; the fourth is to ensure that research is founded upon local perceptions of problems; and the fifth is to ensure that research emphasizes "reasonable goals" and "appropriate means" that "maximize local involvement and participation." These components, once satisfied, mean that a broader community goal has been realized. As another internal publication—Walpole Island Heritage Centre Occasional Paper No. 11, 1987—explains:

> No longer passive observers of the development process occurring all around our reserve and of the environmental deterioration that has often resulted, our band is now equipping itself with the necessary information to assess development proposals and measure environmental impact. As a result, we are better able to meet the challenge of environmental threats from within our community and to take our rightful place as an equal partner in the environmental planning process for projects that may threaten it from beyond.

As this view indicates, the Heritage Centre actively addresses environmental projects that are oriented around three goals: (1) to preserve and restore Walpole Island's natural and cultural heritage; (2) to restore Aboriginal rights and to improve the capacity to manage and govern the traditional home of the Walpole Island First Nation fairly, effectively, and efficiently; and (3) to promote the sustainable economic development of Walpole Island. These goals address the deterioration of rights and resources on Walpole Island, appealing to local values that emphasize the importance of having a collective and coherent vision of how the community can control its future.

The Heritage Centre's objectives are stated in its plan (the Walpole Island Heritage Centre Organizational Plan, n.d.). These objectives include the following:

1. Conduct research on the environment, culture, and First Nation management and governance (self-government);
2. Based on this research, advise Council and the community on preservation, management, and development options for the Walpole Island First Nation;
3. On direction of Council and the community, monitor both internal and external activities that affect the environment, cultural heritage, and the management of the Walpole Island First Nation;
4. Communicate to Council and the community information concerning its research and development work, including findings, policy options, and evaluations of these policy options;
5. Support the advocacy efforts of Council in promoting measures to preserve, manage, and develop the Walpole Island First Nation;
6. Meet the preceding objectives in the most cost-effective and efficient way, through the proper management of the Centre's human, financial, and information resources.

These objectives are integrated into an organizational structure that involves: a Research and Development Division responsible for research and monitoring environmental degradation; a Communications Division responsible for disseminating research and information to council, the community, and outside stakeholders; an Advocacy Support Division that promotes research efforts and assists the chief and council in their advocacy efforts; and a secretariat/administration that provides management services. When an issue or project is identified as being important to the community, it is within the Heritage Centre's mandate to make a preliminary analysis that includes historical and technical research. The resulting recommendations offer options that the standing committee, made up of three councilors and five community members, reviews before presenting it to the chief and council for commentary, response, and direction. If the chief and council concur, then the recommendations are implemented and the subsequent results are delivered to the community.

The Heritage Centre identifies issues, conducts research, and makes recommendations to the outside world with regard to local concerns. For example, it has recently initiated a "traditional ecological knowledge" project to explore the views of community elders. The manifest goal is to accumulate a body of knowledge on the history of the community, traditional medicines, hunting practices, and ancestral land claims. However, this project also fills an acknowledged void in the local culture—a place where respect for elders can be acknowledged and celebrated.

The Heritage Centre has played a part in producing over twenty-four research papers that detail different facets of life on Walpole Island. In addition, there are a number of videos on topics ranging from basket weaving to sustaining Walpole's natural resources. Conferences have been held, and an environmental waste management manual and an environmental audit model have been produced. These accomplishments have not gone unnoticed by other First Nations, and it is not surprising that visitors come to the Heritage Centre for several days at a time to gain insight into how to build their own programs and/or facilities. When I asked Dean (recall that Dean is the director of the Heritage Centre) to contemplate its role-model status, he said:

> A lot of First Nations believe that we are out on the cutting edge, but we are so close to this work as a community that a lot of times we don't realize that headway is being made and doors are being opened. We are creating a model for other communities—not just other First Nations, but rural and smaller communities—about what can be done and how to organize in environmental advocacy.

As well as providing a formal network for delegating responsibility with regard to environmental protection and communication, the Heritage Centre provides an important informal network. I asked Heritage Centre employee Mike Williams to relate to me how this informal network works on an everyday basis.

> I have been called many times to look at different bugs and fish. People have kept something and I'll try to get it analyzed. If I'm at a hockey game, they might tell me they saw a white pelican or something that isn't around here normally. I've got some wild rice sitting over in the corner that resource protection people found and harvested. They [community members] know what we do, and they know if they bring something up here then we'll do our best to try to tell them what it is. A lot of it is research, but a lot of it goes outside the realm of research. A good example might be recycling: We tried to educate the community and we have a little office recycling program going and the supermarket took it upon itself to fill that void. When they started their program they came to us and we had all kinds of info about the support that recycling would get here and all that kind of stuff. So, it is doing research and then finding out what's going to happen to that research, where it is going to go; is it going to go to public works or economic development, or to chief and council for their further direction? We aren't a business set up to make money or start businesses. We look at research issues that the community and chief and council bring up.

Both formal and informal networks are important because, while the former puts into practice the Centre's mandate, the latter informs residents about its work. The use of the community newspaper (*Jibkenyan*), oral presentations, newsletters, and an open-door policy have validated the Heritage Centre's place in the community. The Heritage Centre devises tactics and strategies to protect the community by presenting it with alternatives to mainstream versions of reality. Basically, the work of the Heritage Centre involves a process of information sharing and feedback gathering that focuses on the meanings that individuals construct around particular issues (Kitschelt 1991).

The Heritage Centre has successfully intervened in off-reserve development projects that were deemed a threat to the environment. For example, in late 1992, the Heritage Centre intervened to stop the digging of a large railway tunnel under the St. Clair

River near Sarnia, Ontario, because of its potentially adverse impact on the environment and land claims. And, in May 1993, the Centre obtained intervenor status to oppose the construction of a hydro line across the island—a line that could have jeopardized hunting, fishing, trapping, and land claim interests.

The Heritage Centre has also played a central role in community protest, organizing such events as anti-spills marches. For example, a 500-person rally with the theme "War on Chemical Valley" took place in the spring of 1992. It included a protest march that began with a walk up the road adjacent to the St. Clair River and ended at the Sarnia headquarters of Polysar, a facility responsible for a recent spill into the St. Clair River. Aboriginal drumming introduced and ended the speeches. The participants chanted "No more spills" and waved placards that said: "I Want a Future," "Chemical Spills Kill," "Not Everyone Can Live Upstream," "Poisoned Water Washes Away Hopes," and "Clean Nation for Our Children." The speeches demanded that Polysar and other companies accept responsibility for a polluted St. Clair River by conducting a Walpole Island health study and committing themselves to a clean river. Video evidence showed the anti-spill march to be a polite, organized affair that was so impressive that the Sarnia police chief commended the community for its restraint.

The Heritage Centre's pursuit of environmental protection has resulted in both it and Walpole Island being held in high regard. For example, the Heritage Centre was approached by, and eventually teamed up with, the University of Michigan to create a pilot program called the Global Rivers Environmental Education Network (GREEN). This project involved elementary and high school students in monitoring water quality. In 1994, Walpole Island received an award for environmental achievement from a local industry watchdog called the St. Clair River Remedial Action Plan. This award recognized the community's "continuous pressure on authorities to enforce environmental policies on municipalities and industry along the St. Clair river" (*Jibkenyan*, 7 August 1994). The Heritage Centre has been invited to host, and to provide a representative to, a Province of Ontario initiative known as the *Round Table on the Environment and Economy*. This provincial think tank consisted of twenty-one members, some of whom included prominent academics, labor leaders, environmentalists, Aboriginal leaders, and Cabinet ministers. Finally, in September 1995 the Walpole Island community received a coveted international award connected to the United Nations' fiftieth anniversary. It was given to Walpole Island by a New York–based international citizens group called the Friends of the United Nations. This group is dedicated to promoting the objectives of the UN charter, and it asked an international panel of advisers to choose fifty model communities from around the world who had used a collective approach to environmental issues. This honor mentioned that Walpole Island was one of the first Aboriginal communities to research environmentally sustainable practices.

To summarize, the Heritage Centre orchestrates community projects and research in the area of environmental protection. The result is a movement equipped with an educated constituency, information, contacts, and access to expertise. Individual skills and ability are developed within the community, making it possible build a broad base for future actions. In the argot of the Heritage Centre, capacity-building has resulted from the fact that, while environmental protection may find its organizational home at the Heritage Centre, community members have increasingly undertaken organizing initiatives and so expanded the repertoire of strategies.

The Heritage Centre has been able to mobilize residents around the vision of a safe and healthy environment. This vision is seen during demonstrations featuring hundreds of residents carrying placards that propose a world in which no toxins would be discharged. In other words, the Heritage Centre is a voice for the community—a place where local values and beliefs are solidified and then disseminated in an attempt to seek changes in corporate practices and to affect government decisions and policies.

ENGAGING THE COMMUNITY/ MAINTAINING LEGITIMACY

Because it is a First Nations organization, the Heritage Centre has had to overcome its marginalized status in the mainstream provincial and federal political system (as well as some suspicion on Walpole Island). The obstacles that this status has presented have largely (but not entirely) been overcome within the carefully defined parameters of Canadian–First Nations government relations. However, not surprisingly, the historical treatment of Aboriginal people at the hands of non-Aboriginal people has resulted in some cynicisms on Walpole Island with regard to any organization that seeks to be accepted within the mainstream political system. I asked Dean to explain this community mistrust, and his answer reflected his frustration.

> We [the Heritage Centre] have got to fight the unknown and it's hard. But if that information isn't out there, how can you possibly get the community to understand the problem? Also, stakeholders outside the community don't respect our knowledge until we have a two-headed baby and dead bodies. However, risk and harm are real feelings and emotions in our people, and I think that this knowledge is the source of our community spirit, which is our strength. It is difficult to reproduce that spirit for someone. You can only talk about it. But it is there. The community has to see progress in every area—on land claims and environmental issues. If they don't, it gets back into that vicious circle of fear of the unknown. [In addition, we hear that] we're not doing anything, we're going backwards and we're not fighting aggressively enough. I think we just need more people to understand the fact that there are roles for everybody in the community.

From the foregoing it would appear that the local lack of respect for the Heritage Centre is related to its inability to convince some residents that there is an immediate problem and that it (the Centre) is part of the solution. However, first, I would say that local criticism of the Centre is not widespread; second, I would point out that there is a great deal of competition between "problems" on Walpole Island, as state support is more readily granted to a "problem" than to anything else. So problems are high profile, easily outdoing commerce or culture as a revenue source. But whereas no one has difficulty constructing diabetes, chemical dependencies, illiteracy, and/or physical abuse as problems, they are not as used to constructing the health of the water or land as problems.

The Heritage Centre must be sensitive to the community's day-to-day environmental concerns (e.g., beach closings, garbage, skin rashes, and breathing difficulties). In the conversation that produced the foregoing quotation, Dean acknowledged this. Still, some residents feel that the Heritage Centre does not appreciate their feelings and concerns. Gertrude, a former employee of the Heritage Centre, is skeptical about its level of sensitivity.

> I became more aware of what was going on in the community when I left the Heritage Centre.... Some people

have never been there. There have probably been more non-Natives there than Walpole Island First Nation members. They [the community] know it is there but many don't utilize it.

I think that this type of criticism is a result of the Heritage Centre being typecast as a quasi-academic research body. This status creates the perception among some community activists that the Centre is not grounded in the community's needs. Connie, a member of a women's activist group on the island, reinforces Gertrude's sentiments while adding an important point that corroborates my assessment.

They [the Heritage Centre] have done a fairly good job. They try and keep the community informed. I know a lot of the information is written in a language that someone has to be educated to understand. I believe that if you want information to get out into the community it has to be clear and concise. It has to say, this is how it affects you on a day-to-day basis. Over the years it has become more accessible.

A young father named Marvin, with several degrees and a history of activism, insisted that the Heritage Centre was not adequately focused on activism. He claimed that "there has to be a place to organize, a place for other networks that are aware of the environment and want to protect it, a place [where communication won't] fall on deaf ears, where people will start turning up at community meetings and be able to voice their concerns as a community." Again, I would link this criticism to the Heritage Centre's quasi-academic status as well as to its ties to the broader political establishment. However, I would also consider this critique to be the by-product of the Heritage Centre's recent efforts to broaden the base of its environmental protection research. The result of these efforts is that some residents, such as Marvin, see the Heritage Centre as favoring research over activism. Nonetheless, prevailing community sentiment toward the Heritage Centre is positive. As Connie notes, "The one at the forefront is the Heritage Centre, they...keep us informed as to what problems are and where the issues are and then we respond as a community to those issues." And Reneta corroborates this view: "The Heritage Centre was there in the beginning. Before the Heritage Centre, we heard about things, but we did not know what to do.

The Heritage Centre program started it and other programs have contributed." The two foregoing quotations indicate the importance of the Heritage Centre's activities being community-based. A recent grandfather and music aficionado named Jack elaborated on this:

At one point it [the Heritage Centre] was mostly organizationally driven, with technicians who were aware of the problem and then political people who would become informed as a result. Between these two bodies, action was slow. Action became faster when individuals within the community decided to take positive, non-violent, action. I'm thinking about the women's circle. A lot of what got these women involved occurred when responsibility was given to them to decide what actions would take place. Then the experts and politicians came in. Communication was shared between the women and their supporters. With the women, there was more of a focus on the health of our environment. When they proceeded to have their case heard, then the politicians took over.

Jack suggests that the responsibility for environmental issues now lies within the community to a greater degree than it did previously. As an example of this, he notes the role of the women's circle (also known as the Women of Bjekwanong, or SPLASH). SPLASH was in the spotlight at the time of my fieldwork because it had taken a leading educational and activist role in challenging the discharge of 3.5 billion liters of treated waste water into the St. Clair River some fourteen kilometers upriver from Walpole Island (see Chapter 6).

THE HERITAGE CENTRE AND THE SYNTHESIS MODEL

The synthesis model (which, as mentioned in Chapter 1, incorporates the best of both the RM and NSM models) enables me to sketch the interplay between culture and ideology inherent within the Heritage Centre's organizational dynamics. In other words, it explicates the relationship between the cultural resources that are indigenous to the community's make-up and the Heritage Centre's tactics and strategies for steering collective action. Dean Jacobs's explanation of the place of the Heritage Centre in the community and its mandate as an organization confirms the synthesis perspective.

We [the Heritage Centre] are an arm of the government so we are mandated by the chief and council to carry out that research in the environmental-land claims area. Chief and council are elected to lead and serve the community and we are hired to carry out the community's wishes. So, the community is reflected in the people working at the Heritage Centre who are from the community. We report to the chief and council, who are from the community, and our standing committee that are also made up of community members. So there is a strong community connection in the work that we are doing, but it is still a small working group. Wider community involvement is seen in the interaction in the programs that we implement. Even though we have been project-based for a long time, we still try to focus on projects that have a lot of community involvement rather than just research producing a piece of paper. Community can be seen in every aspect of research. In the past, research was undertaken where we were the subject, but in the last twenty years we have moved to being the principal investigator. We have come a long way in understanding and being comfortable with research. Research has almost become an institution in the community. The Heritage Centre itself might be called an institution.... Over the last twenty-three years that I have worked at the Heritage Centre we have had special interest groups, such as the women or the youth, that have rallied around environmental issues from time to time. These groups came to the forefront when the community has needed leadership and support. I think that is pretty much the way that our culture works; everybody is equal and when there is a crisis then leadership surfaces to the top. That is in spite of having an elected chief and council. The chief and council are there as part of the democracy of our people, but a lot of things haven't happened through their leadership until the community gets actively involved. I think of the chief and council as caretakers until they get the community to galvanize around an issue and move things.

Dean's description of the Heritage Centre's role in the community combines the contemporary political reality of chief and council with the seemingly timeless notion of the value of consensus. The result is a community-based responsiveness that is "structured" into the day-to-day operations of the Centre. This structure has an organic quality that has led to the emergence of youth and women as movement leaders. And indeed, as the following chapters make clear, youth and women have become very prominent in the fight to keep the St. Clair River clean.

3

The Toxic Blob

*Culture, history and tradition are one to me and they have always been
there with me so I don't distinguish them…. In some ways the way we
lived a long time ago and how I was brought up are the same. We always knew that we had to care for everything that was given to us and
to respect Mother Earth and our medicines.*

Gina, grandmother and traditionalist

A tremendous impetus for the Heritage Centre to continue
the mainstream scientific research upon which it had embarked
was created by the discovery in 1985 of a massive accumulation of
toxic chemicals in the St. Clair River. In September of 1985, a fifty-
four-ton Dow Chemical spill became public. The now infamous
"toxic blob" was created when 11,000 liters of toxic dry-cleaning
fluid was spilled into the St. Clair River. It was reported that a
5,000- to 6,000-gallon leak from a faulty valve in a pipeline assembly led to a concentration of a cancer-causing chemical called per-
chlorethylene. This fluid combined with other chemicals, such as
dioxin, to create a "black ooze" that was about the size of a basket-
ball court. Some Walpole Island residents explained the immediate
effects of the blob, referring to an "oily film on their skin" or "float-
ing beads on coffee" (*Jibkenyan*, 17 September 1986).

One of the early results of the spill was that the residents of
Wallaceburg (a mid-sized town of 10,000 people that is located
twenty minutes east of Walpole) and Walpole Island were ad-
vised by a professor of genetics at the University of Western Ontario to drink bottled water. An editorial in the same paper that
carried the professor's warning asserted that the St. Clair River
area was only "a small accident away from a potential disaster"
(*Chatham Daily News*, 9 September 1985). As a result of community fears, the Walpole Island Band Council decided to "truck in"
water for drinking and cooking purposes, and a temporary filtration system was installed at the water treatment plant to remove

"chemical and organic matter" (*Jibkenyan*, 15 November 1985). In addition to news of the existence of the blob, other media reports suggested the possibility that the St. Clair River and the nearby groundwater was being polluted by 2.6 billion gallons of toxic liquid waste. This concern was reinforced by a report that Ontario environmental officials had known about the existence of dioxins in the river for ten years (*Toronto Star*, 4 November 1985). This waste had been injected into oil and gas wells adjacent to the St. Clair River between 1958 and 1976 (when it was outlawed), and now there was a possibility that it was leaking into the river and/or the groundwater supply. Another article in the *Chatham Daily News* (1 November 1985) reported that Dow may have continued this practice until 1984. The issue of stored contaminants in the abandoned oil and gas wells along the St. Clair River has re-emerged at different times (cf. *Jibkenyan*, 13 October 1989, 8).

Emerging fears were exacerbated by the aforementioned geneticist who explained that two recent (1982 and 1983) government reports had found trace amounts of thirteen dangerous chemicals in the waters of the St. Clair River adjacent to Walpole Island and Wallaceburg (*Wallaceburg News*, 16 October 1985). In November of that same year, Greenpeace became involved and suggested that the Ontario Ministry of the Environment knew that "the St. Clair Riverbed contained 'globs' of chemicals" (*Chatham Daily News*, 7 November 1985). Interestingly, four Greenpeace demonstrators had just spent two days protesting the dumping of chemicals by the corporations that resided along the St. Clair River. They did so by putting up and maintaining a banner that was attached to the Blue Water Bridge, which connects Port Huron (Michigan) and Sarnia (Ontario).

The toxic blob led to the creation of a citizens action group that referred to itself as the Wallaceburg Citizens Coalition for Clean Water (WCCCW). WCCCW was primarily organized around the single issue of having a water pipeline extend directly from Lake Huron to Wallaceburg, bypassing the St. Clair River.[1] At the orga-

---

1. In 1988, members of the Wallaceburg Citizens Coalition for Clean Water went to Ottawa to offer input to the federal government's proposed environmental protection act. Included in this group was a resident of Walpole Island named Fred, who has maintained a high profile in these matters (*Wallaceburg News*, 20 January 1988). Wallaceburg has been content to let Walpole Island do much of the work regarding water-quality issues. In fact, in 1990 the Wallaceburg Town Council decided that the Walpole Island Council had the authority to speak for Wallaceburg on matters pertaining to the St. Clair River.

nizational meeting, a recently hired environmental researcher who was working for the Heritage Centre reminded those in attendance that the residents of Walpole Island "will still be swimming, fishing and boating in the St. Clair" whether there was a pipeline or not. Her point, of course, was that the Walpole Island community was concerned about cleaning up the river, not just having safe drinking water (*Wallaceburg Courier Press*, 27 November 1985).

The toxic blob aroused fears of toxic contamination at a time when many people in the community still drew their water directly from the St. Clair River's channels. The hiring of an environmental specialist named Lori Montour led to her writing many of the articles that were published in the *Jibkenyan*. In accessible terms, she was able to explain some very complex issues to the residents of Walpole Island. This gave the residents access to mainstream scientific arguments. The toxic blob resulted in the International Joint Commission listing the St. Clair River as an "area of concern." This led to an agreement between the premier of Ontario and the governor of Michigan to create a bi-national remedial action plan (RAP). RAP involves federal, provincial, and state authorities in information gathering and assessment activities on the St. Clair River. Part of RAP's mandate was to initiate public participation, and this led to the emergence of a Bi-National Public Advisory Committee (BPAC). BPAC was comprised of volunteers who worked for the improvement of the river's quality. It was an extension of RAP, and its role was to advise the latter. Walpole Island officials and residents contributed to BPAC in the past.

SCIENCE FOR THE ANGRY: IS RESEARCH SUFFICIENT?

By the time of the toxic blob, the Heritage Centre had sampled the water for bacteria and the runoff from agriculture for potentially harmful chemicals and organic contaminants. It had monitored the air for contaminants, the land for erosion, and the trees for growth. It had started to report on the number and type of chemical spills that were occurring, explaining to residents the level of risk involved for waterfowl and fish. In addition, researchers investigated the history of economic activities associated with the environment as well as the threats to it. These mainstream scientific ventures were complemented by organized community outings (such as hikes to identify the flora and fauna that were physical features of the community culture). These activities, seen in the context of sustainability, are suggestive of mainstream efforts to detect, clean up, and reintroduce. However, this definition of sustainability did not wholly resonate with the residents of Walpole Island. In my view, merely monitoring and documenting degradation alienates Walpole Island residents because scientific activity tends not to speak to their cultural concerns. Furthermore, at a time when there is a growing awareness of land claims and jurisdictional issues, there is a problem with identifying the environmental integrity of the land solely according to the tenets of Western science. This emerging consciousness was enough to foster skepticism regarding both the Heritage Centre's efforts and the presumed legacy of stewardship.

In terms of skepticism regarding the Heritage Centre's efforts, the toxic blob led to the community demanding that the Centre's emphasis on scientific research be expanded to include community advocacy and activism (which was already evident in neighboring Wallaceburg). Community activism was necessary because (1) the contents of the blob were not immediately known; (2) water had to be "trucked in"; and (3) corporations had hidden their activities. As adult educator Brent, a father and traditionalist, explains:

> About ten years ago, at that time of the blob, a sense of urgency and the need to network was evoked. A sense of terror was also evoked with the realization that there were direct health impacts on kids that were being born during that time. The blob was an after-the-fact response, but the community learned that there was the possibility of *diverting the decisions* that lead to spills. (emphasis mine)

As Brent's comments illustrate, the toxic blob incident did more than just introduce toxic contamination and the practice of legally dumping waste into the St. Clair River. Community fears with regard to toxic contamination were inextricably tied to values that saw the spills as an affront to traditional relationships between the human and non-human worlds as well as to values that emphasized the need to keep local control over cultural development. Before this can be sufficiently understood, it is necessary to know something of the human history of Walpole Island.

A BRIEF HISTORY OF WALPOLE ISLAND

According to tradition, Walpole Island was a chosen ground within the massive east-west migration of the community's ancestors. This migration, which began around AD 900 and lasted 500 years, was predicted by seven prophets and elders at a time when large numbers of bands were settled up and down the east coast of North America. Each of the seven prophets had a prophecy, and each prophecy was known as a Fire. The First Fire predicted that migration must occur or death would result. And death was, indeed, the result of the colonization of North America.

The First Fire, notably referring to the emergence of distinct Ojibway, Ottawa, and Potawatomi nations from the Anishinabe peoples, asserts that Walpole Island is connected to the Second Fire. The Second Fire describes a time when Anishinabe strength would diminish due to a general spiritual wandering that would lead the migrating groups to wrongly interpret their fourth resting place on the journey westward. Fortunately, a boy would point to "stepping stones" that would lead the people back to their sacred traditions. Based on a path set out by the stepping stones, the migrating people would go back to Walpole Island (the original destination) in order to pick up the proper trail for their journey. In other words, Walpole Island is the place where the Anishinabe prophecies were reinvigorated. It was a transition point between the Second and Third Fire, and its existence enabled the Anishinabe to find the path to their chosen ground.

About 8,000 years ago, when migrating caribou herds began disappearing, the nomadic Native peoples living in the area of present-day Walpole Island had to begin "a seasonal pattern of hunting, fishing and gathering" that continued over the next 2,000 years (NIN.DA.WAAB.JIG 1989, 1). This seasonal lifestyle was based upon demands for food, which included an abundance of birds (e.g., turkey, geese, and ducks); fish (e.g., pickerel, pike, bass, and catfish); and large mammals (e.g., deer and elk) that were available at different periods during the year. It was primarily the movement of deer that dictated seasonal migration, and, as winter began, the primordial residents of Walpole Island would disperse into small family-type units to seek sustenance and respite from the cold.

These ancient people also seasonally located themselves on present-day Walpole Island in order to enjoy the benefits of an extensive trade route connecting Native populations in central Ohio to those in Michigan by way of the Great Lakes. The resulting contact meant that exotic commodities such as seashells, copper, silver, and ceramics were introduced, as were the stratification of societies and extensive religious rituals (NIN.DA.WAAB.JIG 1989, 3). Approximately 2,000 years ago the aforementioned trade led to the introduction of the concept of horticulture and crops such as gourds, squash, and (later) corn. The result was the slow emergence of, and commitment to, a primarily sedentary lifestyle. Society developed and was refined until approximately 600 years ago.

The people who inhabited Walpole Island during this period are known to archeologists as the Younge. The Younge were an ancient Central Algonkian–speaking people related to the ancient Sauk, Fox, and Kickapoo populations (NIN.DA.WAAB.JIG 1989, 4). They remained in the area until as late as the sixteenth century, when they were either absorbed or dispersed by the Neutral, who hoped to dominate the fur trade (VanWyck 1992, 149; NIN.DA. WAAB.JIG 1989; Trigger 1985). However, the wars between the Iroquois and the Huron soon led to the disappearance of the Neutral (with whom some Huron groups had taken refuge) from Walpole Island (VanWyck 1992, 152). The Iroquois began these wars against the Huron primarily because of the latter's favorable land holdings (Good 1995). In addition, the Huron were particularly active in trade and acted as facilitators between various First Nations and the French. As a consequence of this status, the Huron became ever-greater rivals of the Iroquois, who were trading partners with the Dutch and British (NIN.DA.WAAB.JIG 1989, 6). Subsequent Iroquois raids on Huron villages led to the virtual elimination of the Huron people, with the remaining 800 or so Huron seeking refuge with other peoples who shared the Iroquoian linguistic classification; namely, the Petun (or Tobacco) and Neutral nations, who also lived in Southwestern Ontario and Georgian Bay.[2] This was part of the era, occurring approximately between 1450 and 1650, that brought with it what VanWyck (1992, 152) has described as the "the fur trade diaspora," wherein inter-tribal fur trade and warfare between confederacies led to the migration of various groups (Good 1995).

---

2. The Huron were also in close contact with members the Ottawa and Ojibway nations which, along with the Potawatomi, eventually made up the ancestral heritage of present-day Walpole Island.

Furthermore, European arrival in the east, combined with Native involvement in the fur trade, resulted in additional stresses which, in turn, led to population dispersal, political and social upheaval, and increased vulnerability to disease. As a result, Native populations were forced to abandon their traditional territories. It was during this uncertain period that the Potawatomi nation moved into southern Ontario and Michigan, settling, among other places, on either side of the St. Clair River. The Potawatomi adopted horticultural practices that accommodated the larger populations of the Ojibway and Ottawa, who had moved into southern Ontario following warfare with the Iroquois. These three nations shared a common Algonquian linguistic heritage, but the Ojibway and Ottawa were primarily hunting, gathering, and fishing cultures and had only limited agricultural practices. For the present-day Walpole Island First Nation residents, such seemingly divisive historical forces as warfare and socio-political upheaval were solidifying, as they led to the Ojibway, Ottawa, and Potawatomi nations forming a confederacy known as the Council of Three Fires (NIN.DA.WAAB.JIG 1989, 7) on this territory. Indeed, the subsequent settling of Walpole Island by the Three Fires Confederacy represents the culmination of a historical fellowship among the Potawatomi, Ottawa, and Ojibway. Historical accounts suggest that the relationship between these three nations is much older and that "they were once a single people" known as the Anishinabe (VanWyck 1992, 150).

CONTEMPORARY WALPOLE ISLAND: A COMMUNITY RESPONDS TO CONTAMINATION

Given the foregoing history, it is possible to appreciate Walpole Island's distrust of capital and its perceived handmaiden, Western science. Clearly, the Heritage Centre's immersion in the world of Western science can be seen as a potential deterrent to its ability to recruit community members. It is easy to recognize these sentiments in the comments of Georgina, a middle-aged grandmother and traditionalist, who explains her concern with Western science.

They say that these discharges aren't going to harm the environment, but these things are not natural. They created something and forgot to consider how it could be made without doing damage. They only did half their job. White man's creation is doing the damage.... They say that these discharges aren't going to harm the environment, but these things weren't created to be in the environment, they are not natural. It is going to damage our environment, our children, and our human resources. I see it, I see that my children can't swim because the signs are up. When I was young, I could enjoy the water as a resource but they can't. My grandson goes fishing but he knows that if there are sores on the fish then he can't keep them. Before we fished all the time and I never saw a fish with sores on it till I got older. Man created it.

Heritage employee Jim explains how residents wanted the Heritage Centre to take a firm stand against the corporations responsible for discharges and spills—a stand that celebrates the Native element of Walpole Island's identity and eschews values that are counter to it.

Trying to incorporate what we know into a foreign process is very difficult because we have to make them understand us and give us an equal level. When we have had school groups come out here, a lot of them say it is like coming into a different world. We don't have the main features of community; instead we have the marshes and the flowers. Visitors often say things like, "You know how to live within what you have" and "You are preserving and not destroying." It is the result of the way we live. But how do you incorporate that into the larger White society? If it is wild or natural, it is a piece of wasted land to them.

In Jim's view, the community's values are not given a great deal of respect because, in part, they express an approach to the environment that is in contrast to that of the larger White society.

An excerpt from Chief Dan George's *My Heart Soars* (*Jibkenyan*, 29 November 1985, 11) best exemplifies the essence of Walpole Island's values:

It is hard for me to understand a culture that not only hates and fights his brothers but even attacks nature and abuses her.... I see him throw poison in the waters, indifferent to the life he kills there; and he chokes the air with deadly fumes.

A poem contributed by a community member to the *Jibkenyan* (6 September 1985, 1) questions the desire of non-Native governments to appreciate the Native relationship to the non-human—a relationship that seeks to sustain the natural.

> Island residents, please beware
> toxic chemicals are in the St. Clair
> Poisoned water is a threat to your health
>
> But water is a very precious resource
> And it's very vital to sustain our life-force
> So is the situation totally under control?
> I guess it is, or at least that's what we've been told.
>
> Is there a set of facts and figures to back this claim
> Does the Ministry of Environment fully explain
> Or are we being told just what we want to hear
> So that we believe there's really nothing to fear
>
> I just believe there's room for debate
> And a cause for concern from which we can't escape
> Those yet unborn will have to live on this land
> And that's one problem facing the Walpole Island Band
>
> Will our children have to deal with it, too
> That just depends on me and you
> For our conscience' sake, let's deal with it now
> And make sure this type of tragedy isn't allowed

Another example of the community's concern over the toxic blob may be found in a one-page passage from John Trudell's *Living in Reality* (*Jibkenyan*, 29 November 1985, 11). It, too, questions the larger "profane" political system (particularly the way in which it engenders racial tension) and shows how it contrasts with community notions of the sacred.

> The current political-economic conditions are affecting our vision of the real world. The corporate greed and political manipulation of today are creating chaos economically and racially. The end result of this chaos is usually corporate expansion and harder economic conditions for the people. This sometimes makes the people forget the sacred things of life.

These passages illustrate the cultural basis for the Walpole Island community's opposition to corporate interests and an outsider culture that abuses the non-human world. As a spiritual leader, adult educator and activist Blaine explained:

> [Pulls out a twenty-dollar bill] That is all those people understand. But look at what is on the other side, who sits there, that loon, eh? They even exploit the animal that for us as Anishinabe people means leader. They follow the green. In the States they say "in God We Trust." In Canada, they don't even trust him or her. Fighting these corporations means understanding how the White man fights, and make no doubt about it they fight dirty. We can look at the river and see how hard they fight. But it is a way of thinking, an industrial mind that they have been taught to do, to put that dollar in front and to forget the future.

At the same meeting, traditional healer and respected community member Ned talked about how the experience of exploitation has helped the community by making it a cultural hybrid.

> We are fighting a White man, and we have to fight him using White man's rules. We need to learn these things. He can only think like a White man, but we can think like an Indian and like a White man. Then we can start using those things that were given to us. We have to do something and not be afraid to do it because everybody is depending on it. The whole Great Lakes basin, not only Natives, but White people and Black people, everybody.

Ned openly questions the community's image of itself as coincident with the "ecological Native/sustainable community" stereotype, implying that Walpole Island residents have lost their unique Native qualities and are, therefore, at risk of acquiescing to Whites.

Georgina, confident in her community's special ability to understand the non-human world, expresses how hard it is to move beyond a cultural comfort zone to the point at which one is able to understand the kinds of values that lead to polluted rivers.

> All Natives have a special bond. I've grown up with it and it is natural to me. I have always had that responsibility as a woman, as a grandmother. It's not something

that was given to me; it has been my role since the day
that I was born. I only know one way and I don't know
about Western science. I can only talk about who I am
and my life as a community member. I think that all Native people protect, and it has always been their job. The
Western way of politics is kind of awkward. Sometimes it
doesn't make sense because they are going to spill anyway; they [the corporations] have their minds made up.

The White corporate forces responsible for the "pollution
problem" are seen as insatiable, desensitizing, and dislocating.
Capital, as integral to a mainstream cultural logic, drives diverse
populations toward homogeneity. This is experienced as a steady
infusion of discursive and practical formations that are at war
with local organizing metaphors such as the phantasmagoric
Thunderbird who, with a violent flap of its wings, cultivated the
deep but narrow channels that constitute the delta upon which
Walpole Island rests. Among the detritus that capital leaves in its
wake are the traditional cultural responses to the non-human
world. In response to this, the community calls upon tradition,
upon what one person refers to as the "things that were given to
us"—gifts whose mention is designed to mobilize a deep connection to place.

How the Heritage Centre Reformulates Sustainability

The toxic blob event was closely followed by the Heritage Centre
becoming involved in legal and political efforts to forestall
projects that potentially threatened the Walpole Island environment. This involvement can be seen in the Centre's actions in late
1989, when it sought a federal injunction to stop the dumping of
dredged materials from the St. Clair River into Lake St. Clair. The
concern had to do with the release of contaminated sediments
that were sitting on the lake bottom. For example, an article at
that time cited the acknowledged existence of two substances on
the lake bed that were known "to cause mutations, birth defects
and behavioral problems in fish, birds and other wildlife" (*Jibkenyan*, 13 October 1989, 1). Walpole Island's position was that the
testing of toxins on this sediment "was grossly inadequate"
(*Jibkenyan*, 13 October 1989, 1). In addition, the Walpole Island

contingent that went to seek the injunction held that it was "their environment, as it had been for centuries and will be forever" (*Jibkenyan*, 13 October 1989, 5). Despite the presiding judge's recognition of "potential risk," Walpole Island lost this case (although it did receive compensation) (*Jibkenyan*, 27 October 1989, 1).

Despite the loss, this intervention and others like it constituted important lessons for the Heritage Centre. Dean explains:

> It showed the federal government that we meant what we said and we were prepared to take them to court over environmental issues if necessary. In doing so, you have to know your stuff, and we learned very quickly that we had to back up what we said. I think that was a good learning process. Specifically, the dredging dispute created credibility and an information process where the federal government agreed to share their information with the First Nation on future dredging operations. We are better informed now about all our opponents. They are beginning to understand that we aren't stopping progress according to some romantic vision of First Nations people as the first conservationists, as some Iron Eyes Cody of North America. There is a lot behind that view, but it is also a stereotypical view based upon a perceived underdevelopment in our communities. This natural state in our community is not about not wanting to be involved in technology, it is about making our own decisions. This is what we have to educate government and corporations about. We thought that they would educate themselves about us, but we can do a much better job because we believe in what we are doing and we have a passion for this subject. Real visible wins are successes, but so is the education of the decision-makers.

As Dean's comments suggest, the Heritage Centre began to enter the judicial and political mainstream in response to community needs. It gained credibility and community support in the process of establishing a collective community identity.

These early confrontations gave the Heritage Centre insight into how community members responded to environmental degradation. This led to an awareness of the possibilities for a radical reconceptualization of the Walpole identity—something that entailed a fundamental and self-conscious break with a colonized and subjugated past. The result: a radical grassroots movement advancing the notion of Native peoples as stewards of the environment and, as such, appropriate models for Whites (who persist in seeing themselves as "masters" of the environment).

It is undoubtedly true that Native values and beliefs have been romanticized in such figures as Iron Eyes Cody, the Native actor who is famous for his role in the previously mentioned 1970s anti-pollution advertising campaign. But in fact several interviewees cried when they were asked to discuss the health of the natural world surrounding Walpole Island. Native environmental justice concerns have refuted the image of Native peoples as a single culture symbolizing harmony with the natural world. Profit-seeking entities have inundated popular culture with books and films celebrating the supposed universality of the spiritual side of Indian life, tapping into the desire of non-Natives to project onto Natives the values and the sense of sacredness that they find lacking in their own lives.

Walpole Island argues for a cultural diversity that clearly refutes the misanthropic views of modernity. It insists on preserving Native human and land resources simply and precisely because diverse cultures form a part of human life. What community members want to see in the Heritage Centre's message is a recognition of their traditional values and beliefs. The director of the Heritage Centre said that if the Centre could accumulate some victories, then this would facilitate the ability of community members to make their own decisions because it would both educate them and provide them with self-confidence.

So it is no surprise that the Heritage Centre intervened on behalf of the community in a number of projects that were deemed a threat to the environment. For example, in late 1992 the Heritage Centre intervened in an effort to stop a proposal to dig a large railway tunnel under the St. Clair River at Sarnia because of its potential environmental and land claims impact. In May 1993 the Heritage Centre obtained intervenor status to oppose the construction of a hydro line that could jeopardize hunting, fishing, trapping, and land claim interests. It also successfully intervened in the construction of a new gas pipeline (that was to extend from an area near Wallaceburg to Windsor) that threatened both the environment and traditional harvesting areas. The Heritage Centre was also instrumental in ending the construction of a rotary kiln incinerator southeast of Sarnia.

The Heritage Centre's ability to be so effective is directly related to its awareness of community consciousness being a cata-
lyst for solidarity and collective identity. McClurg Mueller (1992,
9) refers to consciousness as "the context of social interaction and
social structure, on the one hand, and the storehouse of meanings
associated with a group or society's political culture on the
other," and it is now time to take a closer look at it.

CONSCIOUSNESS NEGOTIATED

The toxic blob, as a critical event in determining the direction of
the environmental justice movement on Walpole Island, led to a
much higher profile for environmental issues. Specifically, the existing interest in water quality received increased scrutiny against
the backdrop of the blob. What also begins to emerge is the collective action frame of "ecological Native/sustainable community,"
with the residents beginning to understand the relationship between the threat of "toxic" contamination and their history of
"cultural" contamination and loss of autonomy.

In general, the point of tying the toxic blob to broader fears of
losing cultural autonomy is that it shows that residents don't see
tradition as static. Here, tradition is about "melting down" stories
and memories that are salient to finally being able to again make
autonomous decisions about the future. The responses of community members to environmental issues on Walpole Island is
deeply embedded in their consciousness of being Native. A response to these conditions must elicit beliefs in a set of responsibilities that are accentuated by myth (the Seventh Generation
prophecy), symbols (Aboriginal sovereignty based upon Aboriginal title), and values. These responsibilities are onerous: collective
activity exacts an emotional toll because it entails entering mainstream life and the social world outside the community.

Consciousness enables collective identity, fortifying "we-ness"
by generating a critique of oppressive social practices because it
keeps alive the experiences of past struggles. Under appropriate
conditions these memories inspire collective social action through
contextualized reinterpretations (Lele 1995, 52). On Walpole, for
example, harm to Native populations is itself seen as an act of environmental injustice. This larger master narrative is the product
of two historical accounts: (1) oppressive actions against Native
people and (2) Native people as the original environmentalists. It

is understandable that, as Lele explains, collective identity is conditioned by "historical moments," specific snapshots of tradition that condition the hopes for a future society. The process of fashioning a collective identity stems from the individual actor, who is embedded in a cultural tradition that shapes her/his personal history and experience and, therefore, the norms and values that she/he accepts as natural and universal. The "ecological Native/sustainable community" identity is the product of shared individual meanings that culminate in seeing social conditions as unjust, consequently transforming the individual self and constructing an identifiable "we." Collective identity is essential to the successful emergence of a social movement. In other words, the fight for freedom from corporate polluters can be placed within a broader community narrative of exploitation and betrayal. In this narrative, autonomy means being able to contain mainstream culture by using what is locally meaningful. The result, for community members, is a heightened consciousness that has the potential to fortify the community's resolve. Consciousness must be seen in the context of community understandings that deny modernity and the actions of powerful outsiders (who sponsor the "naturalness" of environmental harm and/or tout it as the inevitable product of progress).

In summary, the toxic blob offers a critical moment for seeing how the Heritage Centre has expanded its activities from mainstream scientific research to advocating for the community's environmental concerns. The Centre uses culturally relevant meanings to mobilize community fear and anger, focusing on the historical importance of cultural autonomy and control. The target of community anger? Corporations as representatives of mainstream, or White, culture. This lends credence to the powerful view that there exists a set of reified forces that work to undermine Walpole Island's well-being. In other words, behind the desire for organizational activism was the perception that toxic contamination was yet another example of Walpole Island's inability to control outside cultural influences. Accordingly, it is significant that the Heritage Centre's collective action frame of "ecological Native/sustainable community" was expanded to include the principle of community self-determination. Scientific research alone was not enough to engage a Native community that was fearful of the health and cultural impacts of toxic spills and the corporate values and beliefs that allowed them.

4

The Pipeline/Water Tower

Community controversy over the construction of a pipeline that would bring water to Walpole Island directly from Lake Huron, and the resulting decision to build a water tower instead, offers an example of how the notion of "ecological Native/sustainable community" solidified itself as the collective action frame for the environmental justice movement. The water pipeline/tower event not only shows the development of collective identity, consciousness, and solidarity, it also shows how the community constructed its "greenness" by tying reverence for the elderly and concern for future generations to anti-discharge sentiment.

THE EVENT

Despite the fact that the federal government had little problem with contributing the relatively small community costs of $925,000 for the nearly $60 million project, the community of Walpole Island turned down a water pipeline in January 1992. While these costs were cited by Walpole Island as one of the major reasons for the pull-out, the real reluctance was best explained by the Wallaceburg mayor: "They've always been against the pipeline philosophy. It doesn't surprise me from that point of view, and I give them credit for standing up for their beliefs" (*Chatham Daily News*, 23 January 1992).

The beliefs that the mayor mentions include an uncompromising understanding of the river as a continuing source of food, recreation, and spiritual inspiration. At first glance it is surprising that there was an ongoing community discussion over constructing a water tower that would provide a three-day water supply in the event of a spill necessitating the closure of the water treatment plant. For example, in May 1991 Walpole Island chief Bob Williams used a public meeting to express the community's frustration

over the large number of recent spills and to garner support for a
water tower that would halt the "trucking in" of water (*Chatham
Daily News*, 1 May 1991).[1] This anger was real, as was made evident in a letter that the chief wrote to the chairman of Bayer AG of
Germany (*Wallaceburg News*, 19 June 1991, 9). Bayer AG is the par-
ent company of Polysar, one of the major sources of spills into the
St. Clair River. This letter reflected the community both as other
and as a victim of capital:

> Walpole Island is not some Third World dumping ground
> for multi-national corporations...Your industries are the
> ones who are poisoning our waters. Last winter it was
> DOW. Last week it was POLYSAR. *Your* system is not
> working. It is *your* system. *Your* laws are not working.
> *Your* institutions are not working. *Your* enforcement mea-
> sures are weak.

A water tower, which holds enough fresh water to supply the
community for three days, was eventually opened in the spring of
1995. The large blue water tank at the top of the tower is adorned
with the community logo and the words "Walpole Island: Unceded Territory." Located near the storage silos for the agricultural cooperative, the tower is easily viewed from the main
highway that cuts through the community. The tower was fi-
nanced by the Department of Indian and Northern Affairs, the
Ontario government, and the community. According to interviewees, the water tower was constructed for two major reasons.
First there was what Island politician Joseph called "the endless
discussions and little real progress in the construction of a fresh
water pipeline from Lake Huron to Walpole Island," which
would have circumvented the St. Clair River as a water source.
Second, there were what public works employee Ned called the
"fears and anxieties associated with water intake closures" that
necessitated the "trucking in" of water.

As the following discussion shows, an educated public was
able to discern the threats posed by spills. This fact, combined

1. Indeed, the community's water supply was closed two more times
immediately after the meeting. The resulting anger in the community led to
Chief Bob Williams's demand for the formation of an inter-governmental
emergency task force on spills (*Jibkenyan*, 26 July 1991, 1). The task force had
representatives from the federal, provincial, and Walpole Island governments
(*Wallaceburg News*, 24 July 1991).

with the water pipeline response, implies a larger project at work, and I suggest that this has to do with a collective identity that is both Native and specific to Walpole Island.

Nineteen eighty-six brought the end of the toxic blob. In addition, the Heritage Centre decided to conduct scientific studies by analyzing ducks and muskrats for toxic contamination in the form of PCBs (*Jibkenyan*, 15 March 1986). There was also a wild meat survey undertaken in 400 households. The results showed that some fish, duck, deer, muskrat, pheasant, turtle, moose, or raccoon were consumed in 91 percent of the households every week. In addition, 65 percent of those surveyed expressed concern over this consumption (*Jibkenyan*, 9 May 1986). As a result of this survey, the Heritage Centre encouraged the residents to limit their consumption of fish due to the problems of premature births, smaller young, and toxic accumulation through the food chain (*Jibkenyan*, 22 May 1987, 4). This warning was especially geared toward pregnant and breast-feeding mothers. This information solidified pre-existing fears of toxins as especially threatening to future generations of Walpole Islanders, and it has become a central motivating factor in the movement and the identity it has helped to cultivate.

The wild meat survey enabled the Heritage Centre to arm the community with important information about contamination and health risk. The Centre was able to educate residents about these risks by showing the connections between contaminants and human ill health. As some resident statements will assert, these measurements and observations concerning cause-and-effect relationships have tended to reinforce the less "scientific" realms of environmental inquiry. In some ways, the increasingly comfortable place of science in the community has also generated confidence in homegrown sources of knowledge. For example, the potential for toxicity was explained using the concepts of parts per million, billion, and trillion. The following analogies were offered (*Jibkenyan*, 7 November 1986):

PPM—1 grain of salt in a half cup of sugar or 1 drop of vermouth in a barrel of gin.

PPB—1 second in 30 years

PPT—1 second in 30,000 years

The concept of biomagnification was illustrated by using a chart that showed four smaller species of fish being consumed by a larger species of fish, which, in turn, is preyed upon by birds. As one ascends these species levels, each is shown to have a higher level of contamination than did the one that preceded it. In other words, biomagnification explains that the level of contamination is more pronounced for species that are higher up on the food chain. The effects of bioaccumulation are portrayed in this same chart by showing higher amounts of contamination in every species over time.

And so it was an educated public that debated the pipeline/ water tower issue. This is corroborated by Jim, the Heritage Centre employee I cited in Chapter 3, who believes that there is a good general level of knowledge about the health risks posed by toxins:

> I think a lot of our people are starting to understand that there are long-term and cumulative effects of toxins. They are asking if what might be in my body that won't affect me…might affect my kids. That is what the community is fearing. There is also the emotional issue of not really knowing what is going on. You can't really do anything to the companies because you can't prove in a court of law what you feel in your heart.[2]

Clearly, the emotions surrounding water-quality issues are powerful. One may see the residents' rejection of the pipeline and the subsequent construction of the water tower as the product of their

---

2. Another argument for community awareness can be found in the community's desire to have a health study conducted. For example, in March 1991, it was reported that the Ministry of Health admitted that its 1986 post–toxic blob study of the effects of drinking water on pregnancies was flawed. This information reinforced the desire to have a separate health study conducted in the community, as Walpole Island had not been included in the original, flawed study. The fact that Walpole Island had been ignored was a sore spot with community members; and the fact that not only was this study five years old before it was released, but that it was also found to be flawed, brought increased pressure for a health study. In fact, there were still calls for a health study in late 1992 at a meeting on Walpole Island that was designed to discuss and provide Aboriginal input into the province's forthcoming Environmental Bill of Rights (*London Free Press*, 2 December 1992). The bill of rights allows greater scrutiny of the decision-making processes that pertain to the environment. This marked the second visit of Ontario environment minister Ruth Grier to Walpole Island that year. She had visited in May to support the construction of a pipeline to Walpole Island (*Jibkenyan*, 29 May 1992, 1). It is interesting to note that the pipeline was not a major objective for the members of the Walpole Island community, as its construction would have compromised their stance on zero discharge and the clean-up of the St. Clair River (*London Free Press*, 26 April 1992).

emotional connection to the Earth. Dean, the director of the Heritage Centre, reinforces this in almost new-age terms, as he explains the role of emotions in community concerns.

> A lot of concern is based on the emotions around what is going on. It gets back to our passion and our ability to speak from the heart. This is our way of talking about these issues in the community. We can talk about these things with passion because we believe in them.

This passion is exacerbated by fear. When I asked Reneta about specific community concerns regarding the spills, she suggested the following:

> There are a number of people who say they get sick if they drink faucet water and they have purchased bottled water or boiled water. So whether it is mental or physical isn't really the issue; these people feel that way about it. I still drink the regular faucet water, and I trust the public works, as does the majority of the population. However, I do believe that there is a real danger connected to spills. It might still do damage to somebody eventually.

In this intersection of belief and illness, fear is recast as the product of a special storehouse of Native knowledge that heightens resident sensitivity to environmental degradation.

ELDERS AND FUTURE GENERATIONS

Because a pristine past is critical to whatever privileges Native populations are accorded vis-à-vis the environment, the spiritual link between the community and the Creator must be established, and elders as well as future generations are called upon to do this. Newborns have just been with him/her while elders are looking toward the afterlife. As Health Centre employee Perry understands it: "The elders and the children are special because they are the closest to the Creator. One has just born and one is about to meet him or her again." Community elders offer a voice that provides context and scale to the considerable social changes that have occurred. For example, telephones did not arrive on Walpole Island until the 1950s, and the bridge to the mainland was not erected until 1970.

At one level then, the presence of elders in the community provides a concrete critique of contemporary Walpole Island. For example, one interview with a community elder named Gladys produced several acknowledgments of the rapid pace of social change. This elder, who was one of two who died suddenly during my research, considered these changes to be a mixed blessing:

> You know, the mall and the nursery school is nice but it is changing, and when you go off the main road you see the real Walpole. It's just that people want more and more and they bring that home from outside.

In another example, an elder named Gertrude had a bleak view of the future: "To be truthful, I think the damage has been done. It has gone past the point of [no] return."

Senior members of the community are a link to the past, and the past always signifies the traditional way of life. This link to the past is the source of the educational role played by elders. For example, older members of the community are responsible for showing Walpole Island youth the correct path. Elders use their accumulated knowledge to educate the young about the environment and its significance to the community. They can offer insights into the changes that are occurring in the environment. In an interview with a dynamic and vital elder named Reneta, I was provided with an anecdote that explained how the local climate had been altered.

> The environmental changes that come to mind are physical changes that we can see during the wintertime. We used to be able to cross the ice in the winter and the ice would be frozen. It has definitely been warming up and there aren't those winters anymore. That is physical evidence of what is going on in the water.

More generally, then, elders attempt to maintain local culture by collecting and transmitting a storehouse of traditional knowledge. This knowledge supplies the ammunition for resistance to mainstream ideas about legally allowable discharges and the need for "proof" before stopping pollution. Indeed, there are signs on Walpole Island that residents are looking for elders to provide them with a "science" rooted in cultural beliefs. As Tammy, a community member responsible for cultural enrichment, explains: "I would say that our community, and especially our younger people, are involved in our traditions. I think we are going back to where we should be as Native people. We believe that we are caretakers of Mother Earth, and these things are in our heart and soul." A middle-aged man named Stuart reinforces this point: "It has always been our heritage to maintain our old traditions because once we lose that we have nothing. When I was a youngster, elders educated people in the community about the traditional ways in order to keep them. This is important because traditions are like the environment, once it's gone it's gone—it'll be no more."

Stuart's explanation was buttressed by Steve, an employee of the elementary school, who saw elders as embodying the accumulated knowledge of the community: "We need to preserve the knowledge we have and pass it on to the next generation. We are guarding the future generation." This rich source of tradition is tied to future generations by the desire of younger members of the community to become as knowledgeable as the elders. As a young college student named Nancy relates: "When you talk to some of the elders, the true elders, those who know their language and their culture and their heritage—they have this inner strength and some of the stuff that they know is just beyond what you could put down on paper. When you talk to those people you realize how little you know."

Having had the opportunity to meet community elders and to hear others speak of them, it strikes me as important to emphasize that emotions play a critical role in grounding abstract scientific concepts linked with contamination, and these emotions are often tied to the young and old and what they represent to the community. No doubt there are those who would say that Walpole Island's alleged concern about children and elders is a main tenet of non-Native culture as well and that it is equally vapid and meaningless for both. The difference I detect involves the role of place in Native culture—a connection to the thousands of years of Native history and occupation of what is now known as Walplole Island. Let me elaborate by looking at the historical developments that created Walpole Island and at how those developments managed to integrate social relations between the generations.

RECENT PAST

By the early 1700s, members of the Ojibway and Ottawa nations had settled on or near land that is now known as Walpole Island, and they set up an encampment on a St. Clair River channel called Le Chenail Ecarte (or, more commonly, the Snye River). This channel today borders the Walpole Island First Nation.

However, a few members of the Ottawa population moved south to live alongside the Potawatomi and Ojibway nations, which had already migrated to Fort Detroit. These three nations had originally sided with the French during their colonial wars with England. However, many switched to the British after the latter's success in Canada during the Seven Years War of 1756–1763. After their victory, the British issued the Royal Proclamation of 1763. This edict established an "Indian Territory" that extended across the continental United States and Canada, and it recognized the territory west of the Thirteen Colonies as Aboriginal. According to this decree, no private persons could procure land in this Aboriginal territory. If such lands were made available for purchase, then the British Crown would buy them according to the terms of a land surrender treaty worked out with the community in question.

Long (1992) explains that this legislation is crucial to understanding the legal and political status of Native peoples today. He suggests that this legislation asserts protection and aid as well as sovereignty. Part of the Royal Proclamation reads:

> And whereas it is just and reasonable, and essential to our Interest, and the Security of our Colonies, that the several Nations or Tribes of Indians with whom we are connected, and who live under our Protection, should not be molested or disturbed in the Possession of such Parts of Our Dominions and Territories as…are reserved to them, or any of them, as their Hunting grounds. (Trigger 1991, 71)

Trigger (1991, 72) sees this passage as central to contemporary legal efforts by Native communities to assert control over their unceded lands. Walpole Island is one of those communities.

After the American Revolution, the Royal Proclamation of 1763 was not honored by the new United States government. In its place, the American government put the Indian Removal Act. Under the terms of this act all Indian peoples were to be moved west of the Mississippi River (Leighton 1986). This act forced Native populations, including members of the Ottawa, Ojibway, and Potawatomi nations, to depart for Michigan and Ontario. Those migrating to Walpole Island were predominantly Potawatomi (VanWyck 1992, 156–157).

A series of land cessions and treaties were signed in the late 1700s and early 1800s, inadvertently constructing the Walpole Island reserve by omitting it from any treaty and therefore, almost by default, making this land available for Ojibway, Ottawa, and Potawatomi settlement (NIN.DA.WAAB.JIG 1987). These treaties included the Niagara (1764), Detroit (1765), Lake Ontario (1766), Simcoe (1794), and the St. Anne Island (1796) agreements. Of these, the most important was the McKee Treaty, which was signed by Colonel Alexander McKee in 1790 according to the previously described Royal Proclamation of 1763 (VanWyck 1992, 166). It was signed between the British Crown and the Ottawa, Ojibway, Potawatomi, and Huron of Detroit and the Province of Quebec. This treaty promised a large part of reserve land for the Ojibway, Ottawa, Potawatomi, and Huron nations, with the Crown receiving all lands south of the Thames River to the north shore of Lake Erie and from a point east of London to the Detroit River. These lands did not include Walpole Island, the waters of Lake Erie, Lake Huron, Lake St. Clair, or the Detroit River, nor did they include any of the islands in these bodies of waters (Leighton 1986). The likely motivation for the British decision to offer to honor this treaty in any form was the need for Native soldiers in the fight for continental supremacy between the United States and Britain (Francis 1992).

Due to their continuing support for the British in the War of 1812, some Native groups attempted to realize their part of the McKee Treaty. Included in this group was the great Chief Tecumseh, whose bones, as local legend would have it, found their final resting place on Walpole Island (VanWyck 1992)—an appealing metaphor for the contemporary resistance to outside control of Walpole. Tecumseh led a Native alliance of 2,000 warriors against the Americans in the War of 1812. Despite all this, a great deal of land connected to the McKee Treaty was eventually ceded. However, Walpole Island remained unceded and eventually became home to the Ottawa, Ojibway, and Potawatomi peoples. The continued importance of this is reflected in the sign on Walpole Island's water tower: "Walpole Island: Unceded Territory."

By the end of the War of 1812 the community of Walpole Island began to take on its contemporary appearance. The following observation summarizes the historical developments and political and social forces that led to this point:

> The formation of the Walpole Island community was strongly influenced by the forces that were well beyond community control. At the same time, however, the Indians' role in, and significance to, the wider society was

never static, and they were sometimes able to exercise and express considerable autonomy in the relationship. Their role in the fur trade (and later as military allies and purveyors of land), for instance, had provided them access to much-desired European trade goods upon which they subsequently became dependent, while at the same time allowing them a considerable degree of control over their own labor processes. Access to fur resources had remained largely under Indian control and was, therefore, relatively open. As a result, Indians were dominated only at the point of exchange, and not in the productive process itself, retaining for themselves a certain degree of autonomy. The same could be said of the process through which they were exploited for their land, and even for their warriors. (VanWyck 1992, 169)

Present-day Walpole Island First Nation residents see the historical forces of warfare and socio-political upheaval as solidifying, for they led to the Ojibway, Ottawa, and Potawatomi nations forming a confederacy known as the Council of Three Fires (NIN.DA WAAB.JIG 1989, 7). Indeed, the subsequent settling of Walpole Island by the Three Fires Confederacy represents the culmination of a historical fellowship among the Potawatomi, Ottawa, and Ojibway. Historical accounts suggest that the relationship between these three nations is extremely old, and it is thought that "they were once a single people," known as the Anishinabe (VanWyck 1992, 150). This belief in a single origin is founded on the fact that all three nations descended from populations that lived in northeastern North America, had a similar lifestyle and culture, shared an Algonkian linguistic tradition, traded with each other, and formed a military confederacy (VanWyck 1992, 149). The historical alliance, known as the Three Fires Confederacy, was, according to myth, formed when the Anishinabe people split into three separate groups. These groups were called the Ish-ko-day-wa-tomi (later the O-day-wa-tomi and later still the Potawatomi [from Boodwenini—a person who tends the fire]); the Ojibway (from Ojibede—pucker), who took their name from the style of their moccasins (which had small puckers around the front edges) and who were the firekeepers and spiritual guardians; and the Ottawa (from Odahwe, or O-daw-wahg—trader people, or he/she who buys or sells), who were the traders for the confederacy (Hall 1983, 193, as cited in VanWyck 1992, 150; Benton-Banai 1988, 98).

The symbolic value of the three fires is prevalent in the community, and it is portrayed on many posters and by many logos. It also plays a role in the renewed interest in language on the part of Walpole residents, particularly women. A number of interviewees brought up the issue of language. In general, the community dialect is an amalgam of Potawatomi, Ojibway, and Ottawa, although there are subtle differences in the pronunciation of particular words. This dialect has emerged over time, reflecting the political and social integration that has taken place over the last 300 years. The recent value given to the retention of Native language has to do with its ability to bond community members to one another. In particular, the community dialect connects the elders (who tend to speak it fluently) with younger people who want to learn it. Several interviewees observed the role of language with respect to connecting the generations, but in general they thought that this important symbol was endangered. Consequently, there are renewed signs of interest in language, as is evidenced by (1) a regular article in the local newsletter that attempts to teach the dialect and (2) its having become a small part of the elementary school's curriculum. Language is a metaphor for the culture itself, and more and more people are beginning to recognize its importance as such.

THE HERITAGE CENTRE'S REFORMULATION OF SUSTAINABILITY

I argue that cultural influences, as seen in both traditional and contemporary social relations, enable us to understand the collective action frame of ecological Native/sustainable community. The Heritage Centre disseminates information that explains the link between sustaining natural resources and understanding the implications of toxic contamination. This led to the community's scepticism with regard to constructing a pipeline. This skepticism was based upon scientific fact and upon an understanding that the construction of a pipeline would allow spills to continue while removing some of the community's ability to protest. Community mobilization was based, at one level, on emotional ties to elders and future generations. These emotional ties "brought home" the abstract scientific information disseminated by the Heritage Centre by emphasizing how it affected elders and youth. This was a crucial step for the environmental justice movement, for it succeeded in adding a concrete local context to abstract Western science. The Heritage Centre closed the discrepancies between organization and community by reforming its practices to include organizing protests. It amplified its growing identification with a history of cultural autonomy. I asked the director of the Heritage Centre to comment on including protest rallies in its repertoire of activities. He said that "the community was really getting angry around this time" and that he had received phone calls suggesting the Centre "organize something that would get the attention of corporations." One of the results was that the "war on chemical valley," officially called for by the chief, was initiated by the Heritage Centre (*Jibkenyan*, 29 May 1992, 1). This event culminated in a 500-person protest march to the Sarnia headquarters of Polysar, a facility responsible for a recent spill into the St. Clair River (see Chapter 2). The community wanted Polysar and other companies to accept and rectify the problem they had created. The marchers left no doubts regarding their concerns over the need for both a community health study and clean water. The resulting media television coverage, in two major southern Ontario markets (London and Kitchener-Waterloo), was sympathetic and extensive.

The Heritage Centre also stepped up its involvement in community programs focused on exploring environmental issues. For example, the Centre interviewed many of the elders in the community, and their knowledge is currently being put together as part of a traditional ecological knowledge project and as an oral history project. A number of projects and programs are specifically geared toward the involvement and awareness of youth. For example, a 1989 spill involving thirteen tonnes of polyethylene glycol dimethyl ether was interpreted by a University of Western Ontario geneticist as posing a particular risk for pregnant women, as it was potentially fatal for embryos. The response from the community to this incident involved the publishing in the *Jibkenyan* of letters from the elementary school. Students complained that they couldn't swim and that they had skin irritations, headaches, and sore eyes (*Jibkenyan*, 26 May 1989, 1). In April 1994, Walpole Island youths celebrated Earth Day by walking and jogging the sixty kilometers to Sarnia in order to draw attention to the hazards caused by chemical spills (*Wallaceburg News*, 27 April 1994). The Heritage Centre also sponsored an environmental youth corps to monitor the well-being of wildlife, clean the nature trails, destroy purple loosestrife, and create a green directory that offers tips on recycling, alternatives to hazardous wastes, and water usage. In addition, a Global Action Plan for the Earth, an Environmental Week, a waste reduction week, and a household hazardous waste depot have all attempted to create awareness and to mobilize favorable sentiment toward the Heritage Centre. Further to this, the Heritage Centre and the University of Michigan teamed up to create a pilot program called the Global Rivers Environmental Education Network (GREEN). This project involved elementary and high school students in water monitoring and water quality data efforts.

SUMMARY: SOLIDARITY AND IMPLICIT MEANINGS

The water pipeline/water tower issue provides an important opportunity to examine the Heritage Centre's collective action frame of ecological Native/sustainable community as it both contributes to and is formulated by the "authentic, traditional Walpole Islander." This collective identity—sustainable, green, and autonomous—is explained by residents as having been authentically constructed by the particularities of a local lifeworld. If we recall the previously described points of Rogers and Husserl, it follows that "belonging to groups," or solidarity, is created within an intersubjective social context buttressed by meanings constructed out of personal associations and existing beliefs. For example, the residents of Walpole Island are concerned with maintaining a unique relationship to their physical landscape—a subjective experiencing of their identity as embedded in an "identifiable" place. This relationship echoes the concerns of a Walpole Island constituency that is comprised of people who are paying the costs of problems associated with modernization and marginalization. Accordingly, grassroots solidarity accommodates both the individuals acting together to constitute a collectivity and the strategies chosen to confront an external world. This way of looking at solidarity resonates with Taylor and Whittier's (1992, 111) discussion of boundaries as separating actors from the larger society and so accentuating who they are. For Fantasia (1988, 11):

> Solidarity is created and expressed by the process of mutual association. Whether or not a future society is consciously envisioned, whether or not a "correct" image of

the class structure is maintained, the building of solidarity in the form, and in the process, of mutual association can represent a practical attempt to restructure, or reorder, human relations.

This explanation of solidarity suggests that part of building community support for environmental efforts on Walpole Island emerges from challenges to the accepted values of the larger social order. This is an element of consciousness, and it emerges from the conflict between traditional beliefs and the order imposed by Canadian industrial society. Consequently, solidarity is the result of the recognition of common interests, identifiable commonalties, and preexisting meanings. Klandermans (1992, 82) defines these as a "socially determined universe of opinions or beliefs about the material or social environment." It is these, or what Klandermans elsewhere calls the "thought world," that provide "a structure of classifications and distinctions by means of which information gets framed, stored, and retrieved in organized meaning-bundles" (82–83). In sum: a community culture featuring values that instill autochthonous beliefs and a distinct Native/Walpole Island identity forges solidarity.

In fact, I would say that the continuing cultivation of this identity deepens the collective consciousness of the residents with regard to the relationship between their social markings (i.e., "race") and their plight. This consciousness is being cultivated by the Heritage Centre, which is attempting to educate the community. The result of this education is that the abstract and highly complex world of toxic contamination has been made concrete to residents—concrete enough to inspire both fear, anger, and collective action.

Through a wide range of activities, the Heritage Centre located sustainability in everyday practices and ascribed characteristics. In doing this, it built the abilities of community members to relate major issues, such as the quality of water sources, to both immediate and long-term interests. The "concrete" goal of a safe water source was formulated by residents as an expression of how their identity is linked to future generations and elders. In other words, Walpole Islanders responded to the threat of toxins by turning to deeply held cultural beliefs.

5

The Wetlands Management Plan: Ambivalence and Contradiction

The controversy over a wetlands management plan is another event that is useful with regard to exploring the development of the Heritage Centre's collective action frame of ecological Native/sustainable community. In this case, the credibility of the Heritage Centre was tested because of its perceived inability to communicate the full measure of the community's message to opponents; namely, that residents considered their opposition to environmental injustice to be part of a larger sacred responsibility.

The Heritage Centre attempted to initiate a project that would bring international recognition to Walpole Island's wetlands, highlighting them as an example of sustainability. In attempting to do this, the Centre advanced sustainability as an opportunity to foster alliances with mainstream environmental initiatives. Accordingly, its collective action frame, which had previously emphasized scientific research, community educational programs, and personal and economic health, was now beginning to emphasize its "ecological Native" element. Residents saw this as the Centre peddling their knowledge of personal and environmental balance for its own benefit, and they articulated their displeasure by rejecting the project. What follows allows us to uncover the values and beliefs that went into constructing the collective action frame of "ecological Native/sustainable community."

THE EVENT

In April 1991 there was a public meeting regarding a Wetlands Management Plan that had originally been proposed in 1988. This plan was part of an initiative to have Walpole Island designated as a Ramsar site. Ramsar is a 1971 inter-governmental treaty that involves fifty-two nations (including Canada and the United States) and that was formed to "stem the loss of wetlands and to ensure their conservation" (*Jibkenyan*, 3 May 1991, 8–9).

The management plan was conceived of with regard to the 17,000 acres of wetlands at the southern tip of the reserve. According to the Heritage Centre, the plan would include recommendations for the collection of baseline data on such topics as land reclamation, the flooding of cornfields, the management of the muskrat populations, the rehabilitation of marsh areas, the monitoring of wildlife habitats and populations, and the burning of the marshes in the spring (*Jibkenyan*, 3 May 1991, 8–9). The Heritage Centre explained its initiative as follows:

> The wetlands area of Walpole Island will be managed for the conservation and maintenance of the unique habitats of this area's plant, insect, fish, wildfowl and wildlife species. By maintaining and managing our wetlands in a more formalized way through the auspices of this Plan, we continue to reinforce the unique heritage that is the "Anishnaabe," and continue our legacy as a hunting-based society. This Strategy needs to come from you, the Community. The Heritage Centre can provide facts and information, but the ultimate decision on goals, objectives and policies for sustainable development must come from council, Elders, our children and Youth, their parents and all other community members of the Walpole Island First Nation. (*Jibkenyan*, 3 May 1991, 8–9)

The management plan was attached to the popular environmental mantra of sustainability. The plan read:

> Sustainable development involves the process of equitable social, economic, cultural and technological betterment in a way that does not pollute ecosystems and irrevocably deplete natural resources. It also means the enhancement of human resources, improving the capabilities of communities to work towards social, cultural, economic and technological betterment. (*Jibkenyan*, 3 May 1991, 8–9)

The Heritage Centre's plan was sharply rebuffed by the community in the form of a petition signed by 400 people. Opposition

CHAPTER 5 • THE WETLANDS MANAGEMENT PLAN • **73**

to this plan made it clear that there were those in the community who felt that it was being imposed from the outside, that community land would be manipulated, and that community control would be lost. Furthermore, people expressed the need to settle outstanding land claims and to discuss the viability of certain practices before agreeing to let Walpole become a Ramsar designated site. As Heritage Centre employee Jim explains:

> We tried a wetlands management plan and there was a petition brought out against us. It was interpreted as us telling them what to do and we weren't hunters or fishers and they balked at it…. They were telling us that the community is the teacher, this is who we are and this is the way that we lead our lives and this is what we believe…. We believe that our views and attitudes are conducive to more balanced lives than other people. So the Heritage Centre was reminded about what the community beliefs and philosophies are and which ones are okay to tell other people.

The Heritage Centre presented the Ramsar designation to the community as a useful collaboration that would accomplish two political goals. First, it would end the dredging of the St. Clair River (which the community believed activated toxins lying on the riverbed) adjacent to Seaway Island by enhancing the international political clout of the Walpole Island First Nation (*Chatham Daily News*, 2 May 1991, 1). Second, it would strengthen land claims and boundary negotiations by showing an impressive level of community control over wildlife protection and revealing the areas in which help is needed. This would enable the community to pursue gaining total control of certain areas and/or to consider the need for co-management (*Jibkenyan*, 13 May 1991, 5–6).

Accomplishing these two goals was contingent upon the community's extending an invitation to outsiders to explore and to help manage the wetlands in the interests of providing an example of sustainability. The Heritage Centre's collective action frame alluded to the unique Anishinabe heritage, which has, as one boat ride through the beautiful area called "the marshes" will attest, successfully managed the Walpole Island resources for a long time. It is a management system that protects and maintains a habitat that provides residents with a livelihood. For example, hunting clubs lease out approximately two-thirds of the available 17,000 acres of marsh area. This provides an important source of income for the community through land lease payments as well as through employment related to guiding, housing, and cooking. Today, the leases are increasingly owned by community members. The remaining acreage, which is available for the community's use, is an important source of food and recreation for the people of Walpole Island. For example, until recently there was a thriving business in selling muskrat pelts. Articles in the *Jibkenyan* indicate that, at a very conservative estimate, the income from fishing and hunting is almost $1 million (this figure does not include the employment income from these industries). It is more likely that, all things considered, the marshes bring in almost $2 million in revenue. The result is that community members recognize the wetlands, the waters, and other wilderness as offering traditional sources of food and shelter for a variety of wildlife and that this, in turn, provides human economic security through hunting, fishing, and guiding. Through its reference to the community heritage, the Centre clearly indicated that it was cognizant of the need to invoke a community identity in attempting to gain consent for its initiative.

The community's rejection of the management plan constituted its rejection of the Heritage Centre's attempt to position its collective action frame within an argument that would have resulted in outside intervention in the affairs of Walpole Island. The community recognized the contradiction involved in advertising the community's heritage as consisting of sustainable practices and then inviting outsiders to manage its marsh. In other words, the Ramsar initiative did not have its cultural roots in Walpole Island and so was not acceptable to the community.

Walpole Island's cultural heritage entails the recognition that the overall health of the community has to do with the well-being of both its human and non-human denizens. The community ethic of sustainability links personal and community health to the environment and speaks to the importance of healing and putting things right. As Cory and her daughter Anne explained: "The health of the individual and the health of the community are connected." One young interviewee named Carol, who was raised according to Native traditions, articulated the community's views on the connection between the environment and the community: "You know Native people have their surroundings and that's part of them. I think it's more family than 'the natural environment.'" The following discussion more extensively explores the community's response to the Heritage Centre's attempt to use the collective action frame of ecological Native/sustainable community to gain support for its wetlands protection initiatives.

COMMUNITY RESPONSE TO THE WETLANDS MANAGEMENT PLAN: CULTURAL HEALTH AND SUSTAINABILITY

It is useful to begin this discussion with the following definition of sustainability, which was taken from a document circulated to protest a recently proposed discharge into the St. Clair River:

> For Anishinabe sustainable development is an imperative. For Anishinabe cultural sustainability is also an imperative. At Walpole Island we believe sustainable development must be defined in practical terms. The people of Walpole Island Unceded Territory and Anishinabe Nation view life in a spiritual, holistic, and dynamic way. As our ecosystem knows no political boundaries, neither should sustainable development and cultural sustainability know any boundaries. We know we cannot do it alone. Only an integrated approach between society and multinational corporations will be able to reconcile the environment with economic development and cultural sustainability to complete the circle.

Larry is a traditionalist who is extremely close to the land and who derives part of his livelihood from photographing his community and its surroundings. He expressed the importance of the connections between the health of the individual and the health of the environment. Larry believes that one should sing a song of thanks for the healing power of the St. Clair River.

> I walk a lot, and the purpose is to show people that I don't have to pollute this body anymore. I've probably had enough money for cars and I know how to drive but it has never become an obsession to me like most young men. I kinda think I'm not supposed to drive a car, so I walk and usually I'm taking pictures or I'm singing and people can see that I am happy. The purpose is to show people that I don't need booze or narcotics to make myself happy, or have the illusion of being happy, and that's

why I do that. It's thought out and also it keeps me healthy.

In other words, Larry suggests that maintaining the health of one's natural surroundings begins with maintaining one's individual health. This idea was reinforced by Linda, a woman who was employed at the Heritage Centre for a number of years as an environmental consultant.

Native people live in harmony with their environment. This means that everything deserves respect. Everything has to be healthy, including the Earth, the air, and the self; otherwise you can't totally enjoy things. Our people have a belief that we were put on Earth by the Creator to care for all the environment. So if you care for something you have to nurture it back to a healthy way of life.

One young interviewee named Bonnie offered a view that complements the two previous quotations:

You also have to heal yourself within and that's why there is always talk about community healing or self-healing. Once you feel that you are balanced then you're at peace and you know your place in the world. Then you can work towards protecting the environment. You can't protect the environment and turn around and destroy yourself. They call the land Mother Earth, and it is our Mother: it gives us everything. How can you say "yes we have to protect Mother Earth" but then abuse yourself with alcohol and throw the beer bottles out?

Native cultures have been popularly portrayed as embodying a set of values based on interrelatedness, interdependence, and collectivism. These values combine holism and individualism; that is, one's personal growth occurs while one remains cognizant of the larger need to balance one's drives with those of the broader community. Unlike Western countries, which are based on a liberal tradition of individualism, Native cultures are based on a striving for a harmonious social relationship with other humans, animals, and the broader environment (Berry 1992, 11–13). In other words, Native culture does not treat the natural environment as something subservient to human beings. According to Kary (1995, 36):

This view of a cosmocentric whole results in a view of the self in relation to all else that is different from that prevailing in the western liberal tradition. Here the individual is seen as the repository of responsibilities rather than as a claimant of rights. Rights can exist only in the measure to which each person fulfills his or her responsibility towards others and are an outgrowth of every person performing his or her obligation in the cosmic order. In such a society there is no concept of inherent individual claims to inalienable rights.

Walpole Islanders are in agreement with Berry and Kary. For example, a conversation with Ken, an introspective elder, unveils this complex view of collective and individual responsibilities with regard to the environment:

I try and treat all the environment with respect. If I eat a candy bar, I put the wrapper in my pocket until I get home. That way I do my part. You have to start the clean-up right here [pointing to himself]. But I wouldn't tell John Doe across the road "well you better give up your drinking or your smoking." It don't work that way. I'm not my people's savior, or the Earth's savior, so this is what I can do and it's [taking] action.

In this context, individualism is embedded within a community view that eschews interfering with the rights, privileges, and activities of another person. The ethic of non-interference is exemplified in the following response, which indicates the usual path that community members would take when attempting to help someone correct his/her mistakes.

That person would be left to do what he's doing until that person did something really direct that required a direct response. If the person was just lost, there wouldn't be any community collective effort, it would still be a lot of family responsibility to make sure that individual is given the impression that they were still part of the family. It is sometimes normal to fall off the path.

This explains some of the difficulties the Heritage Centre had with regard to interesting community members in the various programs, events, and protests that provide the groundwork for the environmental justice movement. In short, the Heritage Centre's advocacy work had to be tempered by respect for each individual, whether or not support was forthcoming from her/him. Respect ensures harmony and balance, and so it is critically important that any attempt to organize collective action be based on it.[1] As Blaine explains:

> As an individual I feel that responsibility, that need for us to stand up for the environment and the quality of life that is enjoyed here. One of the things that the trees and lands need is human intervention to stand up for them. At one time, it wasn't absolutely necessary because we were dependent on the earth. We have to take care of the land as we know it. Not necessarily as a shepherd–sheep servant–master relationship. It is seeing ourselves as a part of nature and a particularly powerful part of nature that must be more conscious of what we do in the present and how that is going to move us in the future. I think I certainly do and there are others in the community that share that belief. It may not be verbalized but it takes a

---

1. Consider again the views from a respected traditionalist named Ned as a threat to this balance. He had the following things to say at a public meeting on Walpole Island. He spoke after one corporation had received provincial permission to discharge and the community was meeting to discuss its next move:

> We are fighting a White man, and we have to fight him using White man's rules. We need to learn these things. He can only think like a White man, but we can think like an Indian and like a White man. Then we can start using those things that were given to us. We have to do something and not be afraid to do it because everybody is depending on it. The whole Great Lakes basin, not only Natives, but White people and Black people, everybody.
>
> We are too trusting and that is what they are relying on. Put these things together and start thinking. If we wait for a great white horse and rider to come into our community and save the day, we are going to be dead by the time he gets here. Start looking at these ways.

The point is that some community members felt that Ned was assigning blame and insisted that this was inconsistent with community values. It was seen to disrupt the view of the community as an integrated unit by showing a lack of respect for previous efforts and criticizing individual attributes. What matters here is that those who felt slighted immediately made efforts to forgive this indiscretion. For example, it was quickly pointed out that Ned had just discovered that his family had extremely high lead levels in its drinking water.

few people to activate others as leaders and then the community will lend its hands and voices.

Accordingly, individual responsibility is based upon a pantheistic worldview that suggests that the "Creator," or "Mother Earth," is immanent in nature. In other words, the universe and the Creator are identical.[2] The use of the term *Mother* to refer to the Earth is quite common in the Walpole Island community, and it reflects the belief that Native people have a caretaker status vis-à-vis their relationship to the non-human world. For Walpole Island citizens, this caretaker status has additional, local responsibilities. A young university student explains how these responsibilities helped to forge her own identity and how she identifies with environmental issues.

I think for a lot of Natives the environment is just part of who they are. On Walpole Island we understand that the water sustains life and it runs through Mother Earth. That's what gives Mother Earth and everything on it life. So that's a major part of who we are as a community. We live on an island and we have marshes. The water affects us so much. It is more than just the fact that we drink it.

Accepting the status of caretaker is part of the honor of being responsible for all of creation. For example, when a traditionalist named John was asked how he praised the Creator, he responded: "When I say my prayers, I go around outside and I praise my Mother. It's an act of respect when I offer my prayers and tobacco to Mother Earth." This commitment to Mother Earth is part of a responsibility to the entire non-human world. Consider the following quotation from activist and mother Laurie:

---

2. An example of the use of the symbol of "mother" can be seen at an anti-spills rally that was held on Mother's Day in 1991. About 100 Walpole Island residents staged the anti-spills rally. It was called "A Mother's Day Rally," and it followed a spill at Dow Chemical that led to the closing of the water treatment plant on Walpole Island. The rally involved a flotilla of water craft that started upriver and moved toward Walpole Island carrying placards and flags. It was organized by two brothers who are involved in a more militant community protest faction that links itself to warrior societies of old. Their message was simple: "We wanted health studies undertaken which would show the cause of tumors on fish and other wildlife they had collected."

> The people from the First Nation have got connections with the land and we are caretakers of the land. To ignore that the land molds you and your people, particularly when you're talking about people who have been here for hundreds if not thousands of years, means that you are ignoring something very fundamental. We don't want to own it, but we want to protect it.

This caretaker status is also described by Loretta, a young professional who was born off-reserve. "All Native people are in touch with their home spiritually and naturally. This is where we are from, this is my Mother here, and I will come back to her and I will take care of her." In short, for Loretta, home is the place we are closest to and is, therefore, the most meaningful.

The above quotations speak eloquently of the caretaker relationship that exists between the non-human and Native worlds. The support for this relationship is so strong that a young grandfather who works as a community educator offered me a biophysical explanation: "There is a part of our brain that says everything is living and if you destroy something that you depend on for life, then you are making your quality of life worse." These sentiments also emerged in an interview with a young student named Charles. He described water as the lifeblood of the community and of Mother Earth. "We got to start thinking about the Earth in general too because if you don't have the water, you don't have anything else. We call it the blood of our Mother Earth and if we don't take care of her, she won't take care of us."

Community residents accepted the maintenance of the natural environment as a personal priority. A former member of the Environmental Youth Corp, named Aaron, describes a particular worldview that sees nature as immanent and deserving of protection. There is an inextricable link between the health of the environment and the Walpole Island identity. As Aaron relates:

> I think it has to be tied in all together, your identity comes from your heritage, and your heritage comes from your land and your relationship with the Creator who put you on this land. When you take care of yourself, you learn the traditional ways. You thank the Creator for what you have when you take something, whether it's a fish or a muskrat or a medicinal plant, it's balancing out. If you take something then you have to give something back,

like tobacco. Composting is a way of giving back to the soil—or even a prayer, so that you maintain that balance. Once you learn how the ecosystem runs, and it really runs quite well without us, you learn how much you could take without hurting anything else.

Clearly, Walpole Islanders have a cultural heritage that emphasizes the relationship between the individual and the land. As the next section will show, the last 150 years have been witness to efforts to eradicate Walpole Island as a distinct geopolitical place and to reduce the residents' intimate knowledge of land, identity, and heritage to mere vestiges of what they once were. Islanders' reluctance to hand over management of the marsh to outsiders must be understood within this historical context.

RECENT PAST

By the late 1830s, Walpole Island was supporting a population that, while primarily dependent upon hunting and fishing, had begun to rely upon sustained and expansive horticultural practices (NIN.DA.WAAB.JIG 1987; VanWyck 1992). The emergence of this type of economy presented major difficulties, including adapting to structured time commitments, the intrusion of non-Native squatters, and additional Native members (VanWyck 1992, 174).

The majority of the Native immigrants to Walpole Island were Potawatomi who claimed refuge based on the earlier promises of Colonel Alexander McKee. They had been chased from the United States by the Indian Removal Act, which became law in 1830. As mentioned, this law legitimized the appropriation of any Native land east of the Mississippi River (VanWyck 1992, 180; Miller, unpublished manuscript). This new population was welcomed to Walpole Island by the existing community, which offered them a portion of land based upon historical kinship. This initial courtesy symbolized the previously described belief in a historical connection between the Ottawa, the Ojibway, and the Potawatomi, and it helped to forge the success that accompanied the Walpole Island community as it struggled to adapt both to reserve life and to a dependency upon agriculture.

The 1840s marked the introduction of missionaries to Walpole Island. Initial overtures by Methodist, Anglican, and Jesuit missionaries were met with opposition, mistrust, and even scorn. At one point, the Jesuit priests had their church and mission burned to the ground (Morrison 1994). The suspected culprit was a young chief and other traditionalists who were angry with the Jesuits for having settled on Walpole Island without permission and for ignoring Native prohibitions concerning the land and lumber that they used to build their church and mission (Morrison 1994; NIN.DA.WAAB.JIG 1987; VanWyck 1992).

The eventual acceptance of the Anglican Church was based upon Walpole Islanders' clear ties to the British Crown and the colonial government (Leighton 1986; VanWyck 1992). The choice of the Anglican Church was based upon political interests, paramount among them the foreseeable challenges that would be posed by increasing and pervasive non-Native social forces. To this end, one of the conditions of accepting the Anglican ministry was that the priest establish and operate a school that would enable Native youth to learn about the non-Native world.

Religion continues to be one of the most divisive issues on Walpole Island. The following comment, from a traditionalist named Gina, is telling:

> I guess for me in the community right now there's a struggle. There's a struggle of identity. There's a struggle, I guess maybe it's a religious struggle. You have your Evangelistic, United, and Anglican Church[es] among Native people, between people who are going their own way and others who are preserving their culture. On the island here we have our Evangelistic Centre and I find that it is unbalanced. The people that go there are saying that what…I guess what some of them have been taught if they went to residential schools. They are brainwashed right now, and they're unbalanced in the sense that they don't know their identity. They're saying that our traditions are wrong. They're saying don't go collect your medicines. Some people say it is witchcraft, and they are not aware of what witchcraft is and what bad medicine is. There is no such thing as bad medicine: medicines are all good, it's what the person feels that's bad.

The traditional spiritual activities of Walpole Island residents were disturbed by the introduction of missionaries of various denominations. Today, the Anglican, United, and Evangelical Churches have a vigorous role in community life. In addition, there is a powerful movement to recall and exercise some of the traditional religious practices that are a part of this community's heritage. The historical connection between religious denomination and nationality remains to this day. Indeed, since the 1830s the Potawatomi have overwhelmingly supported the Methodist Church. In part, this is because the church was located in the back settlement, as was the majority of the Potawatomi population. The Ojibway and Ottawa populace has chosen the Anglican Church (NIN.DA.WAAB.JIG 1987). The introduction of a more fundamentalist strain in religious activities led to the building of the Evangelical Centre, a church, in 1956–1957. This created controversy when members of the Anglican congregation followed their priest when he switched his allegiance to the Evangelical Centre. This Centre is more movement than church and appears not to be connected to any specific denomination (NIN.DA.WAAB.JIG 1987). Residents call the road where this church and many of its parishioners are located "Little Bethlehem."

The Evangelical Centre is still a source of tension today. In particular, the traditionalist element in the community is generally critical of the fundamentalists on the island and vice versa. This tension is reflected in the opinions of Glenna, a young grandmother who pursues a traditional way of life:

> Native ways are coming back and I think that brings some fear to the evangelistic people here on Walpole. These people [traditionalists] who are reawakening, it's a good feeling for them, and these people [evangelistic] are becoming real fearful. The greatest fear is in yourself, that's what it is with these people. Like I said, I don't want to label them in a bad way: it is just that that is what I see—that is what it is, fear in themselves.

In fact, the tension around spiritual practices led one interviewee, Carla, to make suggestions regarding the course of future interviewing:

> You've got to be very cautious when you go up there to do your interview. You might offend somebody's feelings and not even know it because you don't know who's traditional and who's non-traditional. I guess maybe, in that sense, watch how you use the word *traditional* out there. I don't know if I should give you a list of the names of the people to watch, but I guess maybe I don't want to label

people. I don't want to do that because I don't want to be part of these people who are unbalanced.

As one couple pointed out, neither the traditionalists nor the non-traditionalists had a monopoly on proselytizing.

Another substantial change that marked the mid-nineteenth-century era was the advent of the reserve system and the passing of authority over Native populations from military to civil hands (Francis 1992; VanWyck 1992). The manifest aim of the colonial government in Canada was to establish full-time, year-round agriculture as the economic basis upon which the process of colonial "education, missionization, and direct political administration by Indian Agents" would be conducted (VanWyck 1992, 223). However, the latent aim was to compel Native peoples to leave their reserves and to become fully assimilated into mainstream society (Francis 1992; NIN.DA.WAAB.JIG 1987; VanWyck 1992). Simply put, the goal was to induce the Native population to shed any characteristics that were distinctively Native. For Walpole Island, the reserve system was part of a series of acts leading to a situation in which the autonomy of the Walpole Island community was severely undermined. VanWyck (1992, 221) explains:

> Shifting policy goals, both long- and short-range, are shown to be intimately related to the changing balance of power between Indians, on the one hand, and European traders, settlers, military officials, missionaries, and government agents, on the other. It was only by maneuvering between these competing interests that Indians were able to maintain any political autonomy at all, and their room to do so was much diminished after settlement on-reserve. This political reality, within which they had to negotiate their futures, was mirrored in the shift from the original British Indian policy of protection and conciliation to the later Indian policy of assimilation and enfranchisement.

Colonial history brought with it a legacy of confrontation, struggle, and resistance that slowly but inevitably resulted in Walpole Islanders losing control over their own destinies. Clearly, the ancestral inhabitants of Walpole Island formed an independent group that indulged in trade and warfare according to communal need. However, by the early nineteenth century the scene was one of maneuvering between a myriad of competing interests in the face of decreasing bargaining power. In fact, trade and warfare was conducted by Native people largely at the behest of outside interests. This eventually exacted steep physical, spiritual, geographical, political, and social costs. Then came the implementation of the reserve system. The Indian Act, 1876, functioned as a mandate for the Indian agent to effectively limit Native decision-making and to stifle self-determination. In other words, the Indian Act was, as were so many other policies, a tool of economic and social oppression. It ensured that Walpole Island residents were subject to a foreign system that expressed little respect for Native populations. Given this history, one can understand Walpole Islanders' ambivalence with regard to sharing the few strands of the past that are being used to revive their traditional culture.

THE HERITAGE CENTRE'S RESPONSE TO COMMUNITY OPPOSITION TO THE WETLANDS MANAGEMENT PLAN

The Heritage Centre responded to community opposition to the wetlands management plan by organizing the Mother's Day Environmental Rally and the Crimes Against Mother Earth Tribunal. The latter was conducted on April 25, 1991. It was part of a conference that the Heritage Centre hosted for the Urban Rural Mission (URM) of Canada. URM is an organization funded by the World Council of Churches, and it brings awareness to struggles for justice, empowering victims of oppression through the training of organizers, information exchange, and analysis.[3] The hearing was intended to serve as a community information session that interrogated local industry, farmers, and residents about possible crimes perpetrated against the environment (Nahdee 1991). It was in the form of a community gathering, and it featured outside arbitrators who would consider the views of various witnesses in analyzing local industry, farming, and resident practices (*Jibkenyan*, 3 May 1991). Environmental experts, local residents,

---

3. Interestingly, one of the panelists was a director from the Southwest Organizing Project, an environmental justice clearinghouse in the United States.

and representatives from industry, farming, and government presented evidence to a panel that was made up of labor and social activists. The representatives spoke for about fifteen to twenty minutes each. Walpole Islanders were in attendance, including band councilors, conservation bylaw officers, hunters, guides, and other concerned citizens. About forty people turned out for this tribunal. At an ensuing roundtable, decisions were made according to consensus, and a list of recommendations was drawn up (Nahdee 1991).

The Heritage Centre also used the community's respect for the individual and its identification with the non-human world to gain support for the Effects on Aboriginals from the Great Lake Environment (EAGLE) project. This project studied the health impacts of environmental change on First Nations societies within the Great Lakes basin. The EAGLE initiative started with the assumption that Native populations are in a high-risk/high-exposure category. EAGLE selected Walpole Island for a number of reasons. First, the community had applied tremendous pressure to receive a health study since being left out of a 1986 birth defects study that focused on the Great Lakes (*Chatham Daily News*, 16 July 1992). Second, the community, especially the Heritage Centre, had an outstanding reputation for researching environmental issues. Third, the Heritage Centre had conducted an internal eating-pattern survey in 1986, and this would provide an excellent baseline for the EAGLE project. The Heritage Centre supported EAGLE by writing about it in the local newspaper (cf. *Jibkenyan*, 5 March 1993, 5–6; 19 March 1993, 3; 25 June 1993, 7–8) and by offering information sessions to the community (*Jibkenyan*, 3 September 1993). One of the more interesting attempts to create enthusiasm and support for EAGLE involved the presentation of a story, part of which read as follows:

> In our community, there was a beautiful beach from which our people during countless ages have watched the sun rise and set. Our community has always cherished this beach, but one day, Young Person noticed that the beautiful beach was no longer beautiful.... As the sun set that evening, however, she realized she was someone and she could do something.... Children on the beach saw Young Person pick up one piece of glass or debris and asked what she was doing.... The children loved the

beach and asked if they could help. As Young Person left the beach that evening a thousand pieces of glass and debris also left the beach and the happy sounds of future generations rang in the Young Person's ears. (*Jibkenyan*, 15 October 1993, 5)

While one cannot suggest that this story led directly to the recruitment of people into the Heritage Centre fold, it does reveal that the Centre recognizes the impact of culture on community mobilization. The development of the ecological Native/sustainable community collective action frame is a product of this recognition.

SUMMARY: COLLECTIVE IDENTITY AND NEGOTIATING TRADITION

The community's response to the Wetlands Management Plan stimulated the collective action frame of ecological Native/sustainable community by promoting the infusion of community values and beliefs. It is possible to recognize this episode as one of the "certain critical junctures" that Snow, Rochford, Worden, and Benford (1986, 478) alluded to in their seminal piece on frame alignment. These junctures constitute a condition wherein "framing efforts strike a responsive chord or resonate within the targets of mobilization" (Snow and Benford 1988, 198). The collective action frame is a product of social negotiation and is, therefore, a cultural production. As such, framing processes resonate with Wuthnow's (1989, 3) notion of articulation.

> If cultural products do not articulate closely enough with their social settings, they are likely to be regarded by the potential audiences of which these settings are composed as irrelevant, unrealistic, artificial, and overly abstract, or worse, their producers will be unlikely to receive the support necessary to carry on their work; but if cultural products articulate too closely with the specific social environment in which they are produced, they are likely to be thought of as esoteric, parochial, time bound, and fail to attract a wider and more lasting audience. The process of articulation is thus characterized by a delicate balance between the products of culture and the social environment in which they are produced.

This explains why the Heritage Centre's attempt to expand its collective action frame beyond the cultural boundaries of the Walpole Island community was stopped. Tenets of this identity, such as the sacredness of Mother Earth and the right to an ethical, balanced, and responsible use of the land, need to be incorporated into the ecological Native/sustainable community frame. As it was, the Walpole Island community questioned whether sustainability was being packaged for public (read non-Native) consumption. The pervasive sentiment in the community seemed to be that knowledge should be offered as a gift rather than as a commodity.

The framing of identity is important for any social movement (Garner 1996, 23), and it is crucial to remember that cultural traditions are not fixed and unchanging. However, Nagel (1996, 69) warns us about "making secular the sacred—in demonstrating change and adaptation. Here the purity and authenticity of cultures can be undermined, again often with identifiable social, political, economic, and legal consequences."

Collective identity establishes a tradition, and, as Lele (1995) reasons, tradition is capable of generating a critique of oppressive social practices and ideologies. He suggests that tradition is "that in which the experiences of all past struggles are incorporated and kept alive. It remains accessible as a source of inspiration for collective social action under appropriate conditions and through contextualized reinterpretations" (Lele 1995, 52). Lele's argument supports the notion that collective identity is conditioned by a "historical moment"—a moment that may be identified by referring to specific snapshots in the area of environmental protection, snapshots that take as their premise the hope that, one day, environmental degradation will end. This deep belief in an underlying equity is often the source of a social movement's drive, and it is certainly present in the context of the environmental justice movement on Walpole Island.

Collective identity is the inevitable result of individual actors being embedded in a particular cultural tradition. This tradition shapes personal histories and experiences and, therefore, the way in which meanings, norms, and values are constructed and then viewed as both natural and universal. One of the ways in which collective identity is formed and strengthened concerns a shared sense that extant social conditions are unjust. This often results in transforming an "I" into a "we."

6

Imperial Chemical Industries of Canada

Culture and tradition, along with history, are the same thing. Tradition is everything that has been passed down from generation to generation.

Walpole Island teacher and artist

The most recent event in environmental protection on Walpole Island represents a further extension of the Heritage Centre's collective action frame of ecological Native/sustainable community. This occurred when different community groups collaborated with the Heritage Centre in order to attempt to halt the discharge of 750,000,000 gallons of treated waste water into the St. Clair River. These groups represented the views of women and youth as well as community-directed grassroots activists, and they brought additional meanings—such as zero discharge—to the Heritage Centre's collective action frame (Snow et al. 1986; Lofland 1996).

TEN CENTS FOR EVERY GALLON

Although Imperial Chemical Industries of Canada (ICI) shut down its St. Clair River operations in 1986, in the summer of 1987 it applied for permission to dump untreated waste water from its phosphate fertilizer facility into that same river.[1] Initially, the

---

1. ICI is a London-based multinational corporation that made $16 billion in 1995. It has 65,000 employees in 200 manufacturing sites in more than 30 countries. Until recently, this information was available on the Internet. Now, however, all sources of this type of information on ICI have been cleaned out.

provincial government granted permission because the waste water stored in holding ponds was threatening to overflow and leak into the river anyway. A huge outcry from Wallaceburg residents led to this permission being revoked in October 1987. This outcry was based upon the fear of dinitrotoluene (DNT), which was a suspected carcinogen, and the existence of an unused holding pond. ICI's application is seen by the Walpole Island community as an effort to effectively remove any constraints on industry with regard to discharge. The community considers this to be a critical moment. And it is a moment that contains excellent mobilizing potential for, and may mark a new era in the history of, the Heritage Centre.

The waste water had still not been removed in 1993, when the ICI plant was sold to Terra International Canada. One of the conditions of the sale was that the responsibility for the waste water remain in the hands of ICI. By this time the holding ponds covered a 250-acre area and there was also an 18-meter (60-foot) gypsum by-product stack that covered an additional 100 acres. On February 2, 1995, ICI again applied for a permit from the Ministry of Environment and Energy that would allow it to discharge 3.5 billion liters of treated waste water. This permit proposed that the pond water be released over a four- to five-year period from a drain located fourteen kilometers (nine miles) upriver from Walpole Island.

This application was ICI's response to an unsuccessful attempt to get rid of waste water through the use of a filtration system. According to Roger Cotton, the ICI lawyer, the cost of implementing and running this filtration system was $11 million (*Chatham Daily News*, 17 May 1995). Although it worked satisfactorily at first, this system eventually experienced problems that could not be solved.[2] The decision to seek a discharge permit was based upon the recommendations of A. D. Little Incorporated— an environmental consulting firm hired by ICI. The consultant's report suggested that discharging the waste water would save the company $25 million. Initially, a provincial environmental assessment board granted permission to Walpole Island, the town of

---

2. The problem was later explained as being the product either of pouring the toxin into concrete cement (which almost immediately broke down) or of algae plugging up the pipes.

Wallaceburg, the Wallaceburg Water Commission, and a local environmental group called Parkway Over Waste to participate in a provincial hearing to determine whether or not the permit should be granted. All of these parties were opposed to granting ICI a permit to discharge its waste water. The Wallaceburg Water Commission and Parkway Over Waste dropped out after learning of Walpole's opposition to the discharge; only Walpole and the town of Wallaceburg remained part of the assessment process.

Wallaceburg's concerns were short-lived. As a result of an independent study (conducted by the Wallaceburg Water Commission) of the treated waste water, enough evidence was produced to alleviate the fear of contamination—at least in the minds of city officials. In releasing this information, the general manager of the Wallaceburg Water Commission and a Wallaceburg town councilor publicly pondered whether some sort of monetary contribution would alleviate the economic harm that the accompanying perception problem might create in the community of Wallaceburg. This perception problem was remedied on October 30, 1995, when a joint press release issued by ICI Canada and the Wallaceburg Water Commission explained that ICI had contributed $1.6 million to the $2.4 million cost of a water tower for Wallaceburg. This donation was contingent upon ICI's receiving approval for the discharge, which it eventually did.

Buoyed by the success of the Wallaceburg decision, ICI also approached the Walpole Island Band Council and offered it a $750,000 donation toward the creation of an environmental monitoring system and database on Walpole Island if it would remove its opposition to the discharge. Following a public meeting on November 21, an overwhelming majority of the community members in attendance rejected the offer. At the bottom of the press release that followed the rejection of the offer, one read: "The protection of Mother Earth is utmost in the hearts and minds of First Nations Peoples. Someone must speak for Mother Earth. ENOUGH IS ENOUGH."

The community's connection to "Mother Earth" was illustrated in "sunrise ceremonies" held by male and female spiritual leaders where the discharge was to enter the St. Clair River. This ceremony, undertaken to strengthen the resolve of the community and to cleanse the water, involved prayers and the dropping of tobacco or sweetgrass into a fire. Tobacco and sage were burned to create a cleansing smoke that people pushed toward each other with feathers. This "smudging" was combined with drinking water from the river out of a copper pot in order to fortify the legal team that was assembled for the environmental assessment panel meetings. The copper pot represents both the physical and spiritual necessities of life (Benton-Banai 1988, 68).

Shortly after the rejection of ICI's offer, a community circle was held on Walpole Island. This community circle was organized in order to allow interested residents to address an environmental assessment panel from the Ministry of the Environment and Energy. Everyone in the community circle was given an opportunity to speak through the use of a talking stick. Many community residents spoke on behalf of the water, suggesting that it was incumbent upon Native people to act as its stewards. There was a particularly moving moment when a five-page position paper, dealing with the traditional responsibility of Walpole Island women to care for the water, was read aloud by Women of Bjekwanong (or SPLASH), one of the community women's groups. The following is an excerpt from this paper:

> Among all Native Cultures, no force is considered more sacred, or more powerful, than the ability to create life. All females are the human manifestation of the Earth Mother, who is the first and ultimate giver of life. In our instructions—"Minobimaatisiiwin"—we are to care for her.

The fact that the Women of Bjekwanong played such a central role in the ICI issue speaks to the power of the "ecological Native" part of the Heritage Centre's collective action frame. The Heritage Centre's support of SPLASH is indicative of its desire to include community groups in its pursuit of a safe environment. When ICI lawyers tried to prevent the community circle testimony from being included as evidence, the director of the Heritage Centre and a lawyer representing Walpole Island quickly went on the attack and chastised them, insisting that if this evidence was excluded, then the Walpole Island contingent would leave the negotiating table.

On September 27, 1996, the hearing board ruled in favor of the discharge permit, and construction of the sewage pipeline was slated to begin almost immediately. Concerned citizens from Walpole Island met with other individuals to form PURE (People United for River Ecosystems) on October 1, 1995. Over a period of four weeks PURE gathered alliances and resources to support an appeal of the decision to grant the permit. On November 6, 1996, PURE organized a rally in Windsor, Ontario, to coincide with a conference featuring employees of the International Joint Commission, Environment Canada, and the Environmental Protection Agency. I was one person among three busloads of people who went to this rally down a hill from the conference, facing the Detroit River. There were members from PURE, SPLASH, and the Heritage Centre as well as elders (both male and female), high school students, mothers, and grandmothers. High school students took signs painted with an ICI symbol with a line through it up to the road and solicited honks of support from passersby.[3] The speeches were accompanied by singing, drumming, and eating. At the end of the protest, everyone joined hands in prayer and then followed the drum up the hill to the bus, momentarily stopping the traffic on the busy road.

The high level of broad-based activity around the ICI issue suggests that the collective action frame of ecological Native/sustainable community has become increasingly meaningful to Walpole Island residents. First, there is the belief that the water is dangerously contaminated. As educator and traditionalist Brad says:

> Part of my argument with ICI is that if that discharge is so clean, then why don't they put their out-take upriver from their factory and intake below that? If they have the comfort level they suggest they have, then they should have no problem with that. When I presented that to the ICI lawyers as an alternative, they said that would require some rights-of-way. It is not a legal problem, it is something else. It was at that point that I realized that the water wasn't as safe as they were suggesting.

Second, there is the belief that the community has to protect the environment for future generations. A lawyer representing Walpole Island suggested that community concern is based on the belief that community members will still be dependent on the river long after ICI pulls up its stakes and leaves (*Chatham Daily News*, 19 July 1995).

---

3. In April, Walpole Elementary School protested the discharge decision.

Third, there is the belief that the community must be able to control the pace of outside intervention, and ICI's attempt to use its wealth and influence to rid itself of waste water militated against this. In part, the community position was articulated by the Wallaceburg mayor, who brought up the image of ICI as a steamroller that had been slowed, but not stopped, by the 1987 decision. This sentiment echoes that of Martin, a former political activist and community educator who had recently returned to Walpole Island:

> It's hard to fight a big corporation because they have so much cash and once you become active and you want to fight them, they fight dirty. It's kind of hard to stop a steamroller; it's either going to roll over a lot of people or somebody is going to have to stop it.

Fourth, there is the belief that the community has a special relationship with the river. As explained earlier, this has to do with both economic and cultural imperatives. This was expressed by a lawyer working for the community: "The first nation [sic] has a unique and distinct status in their reliance on the river to sustain their traditional way of life and their economy" (*London Free Press*, 17 May 1995).

These four beliefs were intensified by the potential for the ICI event to lead to a new series of legally allowable, potentially damaging discharges. This led the Heritage Centre, with full community support, to add zero discharge to its collective action frame. Zero discharge attempts to change the relationship between corporation and community by using the notion of *reverse onus*. Reverse onus asserts that the burden of proof must be placed on the petrochemical manufacturers; that is, it is up to them to prove that their products are safe.[4] The notion of zero discharge has been circulating within the Walpole Island community for some years, as the following excerpt from the *Jibkenyan* reveals: "Money does not solve the problem. It's zero discharge that we will be

---

4. This is also referred to as the *precautionary standard*. The precautionary standard reacts to contamination ex post facto (Gilbertson 1991; Fox 1994). This means that environmental decision-making is "aimed at protecting or restoring a resource based on an erroneous causal relationship [rather than on delaying] the decision for one or two decades and thereby risk[ing] losing the entire resource" (Fox 1994).

happy with" (*Jibkenyan*, 29 May 1992). A closer look at the source of these beliefs will show how the Heritage Centre's collective action frame of ecological Native/sustainable community accommodated community demands for zero discharge.

THE COLLECTIVE ACTION FRAME

The Heritage Centre's interest in zero discharge has its roots in Chief Dan Miskokoman's 1993 call for the imprisonment of polluters (*Jibkenyan*, 14 May 1993, 1). The anger in this call was intensified by the events of early 1994: halfway through February there had already been ten spills. This led to the chief and council closing the water treatment plant.[5] The decision to maintain the closure of Walpole Island water intakes, while those at Wallaceburg remained open, was explained as a community statement of protest, and it was accompanied by the following message: "Enough is enough, and it is now necessary for us to deliver our message directly to the environmental violators at Chemical valley" (*London Free Press*, 10 February 1994). At this time, the *Jibkenyan* published a poem from a resident—a poem that offers insight into community sentiment and reveals the level of support for zero discharge.

At a steady pace she flows with rhythm and with grace. Beautiful from a distance, refreshing, filled with life. At one time willing to give—sharing her own. It's a shame that something so beautiful and so tame, will slowly die. She'll never be the same. I often wonder—will there ever be a solution? The only thing I can come up with is PUT A STOP TO POLLUTION. (*Jibkenyan*, 14 May 1993, 1)

---

5. They demanded that Dow pay for water to be trucked in until a third party determined the safety of the St. Clair River. Dow complied with this request for two days and then stopped, citing the cost of $17,000 to $20,000 per day as prohibitive and unnecessary. Nevertheless, Walpole Island officials kept their water treatment intakes closed for a week, at an estimated cost of $30,000 per day. A meeting with the president of Dow was tentatively scheduled five days after the spill. Demonstrators and road signs were awaiting his arrival, but the president did not show until a meeting three days later. At that meeting it was agreed to have a third party test the water, but there was no resolution as to who would pay for the water that had been trucked in for over a week (*London Free Press*, 15 January 1992).

In May of 1994, a Zero Spills Rally was attended by 100 people under rainy and cold conditions, and the protesters marched to the Polysar building in downtown Sarnia (*London Free Press*, 9 May 1994). One resident explained his attendance in the following way: "We want people to be aware of the problem. Encourage the government to help us stop this. Create awareness. We want to make industry realize what they are doing and let them know they are being watched. We'll be here as long as they are" (*Wallaceburg Courier Press*, 11 May 1994). At this rally, the chief reiterated his calls for the imprisonment of the executives of corporations responsible for spills, and he emphasized the need to put people before profits.[6]

The popularity of these sentiments within the community gave the Heritage Centre the opportunity to engage residents with a simple message—one that touched a nerve in the community. Consider the following message that the Heritage Centre published in the local paper to solicit support for early efforts to combat the discharge permit: "Community involvement and support is essential as we continue to pursue our stand for 'ZERO DISCHARGE'" (*Jibkenyan*, 29 March 1996). Community involvement and support manifested itself in a number of ways. Following the publication of this message, the community women's group emerged, as did the sunrise ceremonies and the community circle. Clearly, the community wanted to participate in the Heritage Centre's efforts to stop spills.

In adding the notion of zero discharge to its collective action frame, the Heritage Centre was attempting to recruit support through the use of a scientific notion that was already circulating within the community and that had, in fact, been the motivating idea behind the Dow and Polysar protest marches. This is an example of frame bridging—of circulating a notion that so resonates with extant values that ideological congruence is assured (Snow et al. 1986). Of course, support for zero discharge is enhanced by collective action. The aforementioned protest marches were excellent mobilizing techniques because they fostered solidarity and

---

6. This rally also included a drum song and stories. One especially effective presentation came from Milly Redmond. This respected community elder, who has since died, talked about, as a child, drinking water from the same buckets that were used to haul the water out of the river (*Jibkenyan*, 13 May 1994, 1).

collective identity through the inevitable interactions that occur during such events. These interactions contribute to the education of participants and result in greater solidarity and a sharper awareness of one's identity.

RAISING THE ANTE: ZERO DISCHARGE

At one level, what is meant by zero discharge is quite clear. Gina describes it as prohibiting any "dumping of any pollutants into our water or into our land." The community elder and language expert Reneta agrees, stating that zero discharge means that "absolutely no waste water enters the St. Clair River." This does not mean that residents do not have a good scientific understanding of this. As Cora explains:

> I know it is a pie-in-the-sky kind of ideal because I have a septic tank, so I don't practice zero discharge. What does that mean? From the community's viewpoint we want the plants to be more responsible and not use the river as a sewage system. They might have to shut down, but the world is not going to end if they shut down. I just think there is too much emphasis on the dollar. That is what it is all about. At the ICI hearings, they said that "if we don't dump this into the river then we will be ignoring the most financially feasible technology." It comes down to "well, everything else is too expensive to do anything else." Zero discharge—it's an ideal, but it says that "the more we work toward zero the less we aren't going in the other direction where it doesn't matter what we are pouring in there and it doesn't matter what harm is the result."

The community's willingness to advocate for zero discharge finds its cultural location in an extension of the caretaker status that was mentioned earlier. The duties accompanying this status have to do with a consciousness that sees no clear division between the human and non-human worlds. Both are social, and neither exists separately from the other. As Madelaine, a traditionalist and mother of four, relates:

> I think the world community needs to look towards a Native perspective in terms of respect for creation, all the plants and animals—all the environment. They need to

look to Native people for guidance to maintain the environment and live with the creation rather than thinking of living on top of the creation: creation is created for man and everything else is below. The world community could learn from Native people the perspective of being part of the environment and living with it.

The cultural basis for the people of Walpole Island seeing themselves as role models takes us back to the Seventh Fire. As mentioned in Chapter 3, in ancient times, seven prophets came to the Anishinabe and left the people with seven predictions of what the future would bring. Each of these prophecies was called a Fire, and each Fire referred to an era in time. As will be remembered, the Fifth Fire refers to the period of White colonization and the forsaking of ancient teachings, and the Sixth Fire refers to the time when children were taken from their families. This prophecy is understood as referring to the residential schools. The Seventh Fire is marked by New People who will retrace their steps to find what was left of the trail. This trail will lead back to the elders and the rebirth of the Anishinabe people, as symbolized by the re-lighting of the sacred fire that had led them westward.

The Seventh Fire prophecy foresaw that Native people would lose control over their destiny, but it also foresaw the return of Native power after seven generations of oppression. This rebirth of Native power is, ironically, made possible by the environmental destruction that threatens the planet. Anita, a young college student, talks about Native knowledge of the state of the environment: "The elders knew a long time ago that we weren't going to be able to drink the water here. That's why Margaret is doing the water ceremony...every month. She was told by the elders to cleanse the water every month instead of once a year like they used to."

Mary, a member of SPLASH, asked not to be taped during our interview, but she used a parasite–host analogy to show the imbalance of contemporary mainstream values—an imbalance that, among other things, gives rise to chemical spills. She saw Mother Earth as the host and humankind as the parasite. The chemical corporations were parasites that did not appreciate the privilege of feeding off of Mother Earth. The parasite was giving itself rights that it didn't deserve; namely, the right to use, abuse, and destroy the host.

The parasite–host analogy is concretely meaningful to Walpole Island residents because they perceive the pain experienced by the host. Indeed, the pain is considered to be an important reason to care for the environment. For example, Carol, a grandmother of seven, was asked to explain her community's motivation for fighting the St. Clair spill. She began to cry. I started to apologize to her, thinking that my questions were the cause of what appeared to be her sadness. But she smiled at my presumption and told me that the tears were not because she was upset; rather, she explained that, as a spiritual person, she had been given the ability to speak for the non-human world and that her tears were its pain. The ability to be sensitive to pain is derived from a community's history of oppression and suffering. In other words, oppression and suffering bind the human and non-human residents of Walpole Island. Agony is the result of yet another threat to the environment, one of the last cultural resources left relatively intact.[7] As Pauline, a Health Centre employee, relates, "My heart is in mourning for the river because I feel it is dying." The Seventh Fire prophecy posits that community knowledge is the only hope for saving the planet. A young traditionalist and drummer named Kevin relates:

> Because I lead a spiritual life following the Anishinabe way, I know the truth. The truth is not in the existence of tall buildings or money and cars. The truth is in the trees, water, and wildlife. You cannot argue with these truths because they are handed down by the Creator and these truths are part of the Walpole Island community. The reason that corporations don't want to hear us is because we are the conscience of mankind. When they hear us speak

---

7. The Heritage Centre has drawn on this sentiment. For example, purple loosestrife drives have attempted to remove this destructive invader plant, called the purple plague, from the community before it chokes out the marshes. Purple loosestrife was a pretty purple plant that was brought over from Europe to enhance the aesthetic qualities of gardens. However, it is incredibly prolific, and it gathers soil around its base—something that is very dangerous for wetlands. A flyer circulated to advertise purple loosestrife awareness week conjures up the image of a killer disease:

> PURPLE LOOSESTRIFE can KILL our wildlife heritage, hunting area, and, therefore, Native Traditions and Economy.

The destruction represented by purple loosestrife offers yet another example of how capital seeks to fill every available crevice of consumer need while ignoring any trauma it may cause to the non-human world.

they know they are hearing their conscience speaking and they want to shut out this part of their being. But we are not White people, we are not Black, and we aren't Yellow. We are Red, and the Creator put us in this place for a special reason. This is to remind humans of their obligations and responsibilities to the Mother Earth.

Clearly, the Seventh Fire prophecy may be seen as a metaphor for the political and cultural reawakening of Walpole Island residents. Many residents allude to the Seventh Fire when discussing their participation in environmental issues: "The seventh generation prophecy can be seen in the fact that our community, and especially our younger people, are involved in our traditions. I think we are going back to where we should be as Native people. We believe that we are caretakers of Mother Earth and I think these things are in our heart and soul." New grandmother and activist Mary concurs:

> Today we are on the outside—we are always on the outside—but we're not going to be quiet. Federal government officials seem to think Indian representation isn't really necessary. Today we, who are on the outside, are saying, "Protect our Mother Earth, our sacred waters." As a woman and a grandmother it is my responsibility to carry the fire, the message that our water is a gift and Mother Earth runs sick and weak. Walpole Island First Nation is at the front line of an environmental struggle, and this is the day of Indian self-determination.

The following section looks at the meanings ingrained in the community's understanding of sustainability and speculates on its potential impact on future Heritage Centre efforts to mobilize support using the ecological Native/sustainable community collective action frame.

THE HERITAGE CENTRE'S REFORMULATION OF THE COLLECTIVE ACTION FRAME

The role model status of Native people has been consciously pursued by the Heritage Centre. As the director explains: "We should not only be managing our own resources here, we should be looking at the watershed approach and the Great Lakes as a whole.

It's important that our community gets back to that sort of holistic approach. We have it here in our community but we need to make it part of a larger system." As the preceding quote suggests, there are two reasons for the Heritage Centre to mobilize support from areas outside the reserve proper in the interest of environmental protection. First, the result of taking on a leadership role in contemporary society vis-à-vis the environment manifests the traditional role that Native people have conceptualized as their own. Walpole Islanders believe that they have a tremendous pool of knowledge from which to draw for the purposes of instruction. Ned, a public works employee, describes the connection between being a caretaker and being Native: "I think once we recognize our role as caretakers, then we can begin to have a rebirth as a Native people. You can see it happening now in some communities and with some individuals. But, it still hasn't happened to everyone and there are still some things that we still have to struggle with." Duck hunter and guide John agrees:

As a community I think we need to become involved in those alliances that come together for the benefit of all. The environment is something that we believe in. It's not only our inherent right, it's also part of our dignity, livelihood, and self-worth. I've been involved in a number of demonstrations and I've always felt that I was a part of positive community involvement in this regard. I think they generate a good community feeling throughout the Island. There would be no greater feeling than knowing that you have come together as a world community, rather than just a bunch of people living in different countries.

The second reason for the Heritage Centre to mobilize support from areas outside Walpole proper is that the montage of values and beliefs that have demanded and received representation in the ecological Native/sustainable community collective action frame resonate with the fears and concerns associated with environmental health risks in many other communities. Like Walpole Island, other communities certainly have concerns about protecting both young and old. This enables the Heritage Centre to broaden the definition of sustainability so that it includes looking at the environment as a community cultural resource, thus situating the Walpole Island community as a useful source of knowledge for those wishing to document the socio-cultural impacts of environmental degradation.

SUMMARY: ALLIANCES REVISITED

The result of such fraternization is likely be contact with the broader environmental justice movement. Tentative steps in this direction were seen when the Center for Disease Control in Atlanta, Georgia, and several Native-rights groups specializing in environmental issues made contact with, and offered support to, the Heritage Centre. Of course, community consensus is essential to the acceptability of outside involvement. But, as what occurred around the ICI event shows, the groundwork for such involvement has been laid.

The ICI event united the Heritage Centre and various community groups in efforts to prevent the discharge of treated waste water. Community opposition took the form of a combination of traditional cultural practices, legal maneuvering, political acts, and coalition-building initiatives. The director of the Heritage Centre comments on the changing face of environmental protection on Walpole Island:

> The Heritage Centre welcomes more community involvement. As the research arm of the government we have a lot of flexibility, but we are still government. Interests groups like PURE and SPLASH are arm's-length and they have more freedom, and I think that creates more creative and risky solutions. PURE is an emotional group and that is good. I think that in the short time that they have been organized they have realized that it is a long-term thing, an evolution. At first, it was almost a situation where they appeared to want to separate from the Heritage Centre, but I think that it came back overnight after they realized that they needed more history and more background, they needed a foundation. Community is the foundation, but they needed the data and the contacts of the Heritage Centre. Instead of the Heritage Centre doing everything, PURE and other groups are going to continue to emerge and that is capacity-building. Instead of government always doing it, and the Heritage Centre is

government, these are initiatives that are driven by members of the community.

As this quotation shows, the Heritage Centre recognizes its potentially changing position within a network of groups and individuals seeking environmental protection. The Heritage Centre must remain flexible, provide educational resources, and be able to incorporate the information it receives from alternative sources into its environmental protection campaigns.

How does this apparent readiness to build coalitions and seek alliances fit into the ICI Management Plan, for which outside involvement was rejected? Heritage Centre employee Jim's acknowledgment of tension over the definition of sustainability is useful here. Recall that the message of no to managerialism, rather than the self-reliant local management of the marsh by resident experts, was premised on a definition of sustainability that was advanced by the Heritage Centre. In other words, making such a definition palatable to residents necessitated a reconfiguring of the notion of individual responsibility that is rooted in a pantheistic worldview. I would argue that sharing expertise about sustainability became acceptable when it was defined in terms of leading a balanced life. For me, the points of tension revealed here generally involve the desire to offer this knowledge as a gift and not as a commodity. More specifically, the Heritage Centre was asked to expand its activities from mainstream scientific research featuring some cultural sensitivity, to more environmentally focused and activist-oriented efforts that highlight the historical importance of local cultural autonomy and control. In the end, sustainability needed to circumscribe the broad-based perception that toxic contamination was yet another example of Walpole Island's inability to control outside cultural influences. This trajectory explains the different responses to the ICI discharge and Management Plan.

7

Critical Findings: Methodological Considerations

The social movement literature advocating framing practices has persuasively argued that individual meaning construction is an important facet of social mobilization. Of particular interest in the case of Walpole Island is the utility of framing processes and their capacity to tie the specific interests of the environmental justice movement into the cultural imperatives of Native values and beliefs. The lesson here is that human thought and action, guided by interests and motives, can alter the cultural bedrock of values and beliefs. In this chapter, I offer my understanding of the mechanisms responsible for social movement activity. Some brief personal comments are necessary to elucidate some theoretical points that intersect with my being both an observer and a participant during my stay on Walpole Island. Finally, I offer some suggestions/implications for policy.

ALL THE ME'S IN METHOD

The researcher must not only be honest about what is at stake for him/her, but she/he must also confront the events and situations that do not find a place in her/his writing. In my case, as I look over everything, I see that I did not give fear and humor the treatment they deserved. Disclosing my fears meant risking embarrassment and narrative inconsistency, as did looking at what I found to be humorous. In my opinion, to attempt to depict either would have been doomed to failure because of their "you-had-to-be-there" quality.

I now believe that we must take ourselves as seriously as we ask our research subjects to take us. This means making a claim because we can back it up with what we see and hear rather than merely with the accepted conventions of social inquiry (theory and method). It also means sharing our information, ideas, and opinions with our subjects, colleagues, and the public.

A sustaining motivation in the researching and writing of this book was my desire to close the distance between everyday thinking and writing; to counter what one early reviewer explained was my naive and unconscious portrayal of Walpole Island through a preexisting, Euro-Canadian model. What stuck with me about this critique was that classifying strategies predispose us to separate thinking and writing. I understand why this person made these comments, as they suggest that the environmentally astute activities of Aboriginal populations pre-dates social theory. And it is true that the community does not conceive of its environmental protection activities in terms of theory. However, I use theory in order to provide a stronger foundation for showing how Walpole Island can teach other communities about the process of becoming politically organized. In other words, I use theory within a context that has enormous potential for teaching other communities about the process of community-based organizing.

I understand the importance of outlining the procedures by which knowledge has been produced, the position and the process by which I transformed the everyday speech and actions of others into terms useful to my research purposes.[1] I am a White male social scientist who, upon gaining permission to live on the First Nations reserve on Walpole Island, came armed with powerful sociological concepts (e.g., social movements, collective action frames, and mobilization). I had preestablished a critical distance between myself and those I was going to study, and I had done this by identifying with the power associated with academic concepts. I sought solace in theory because I was ignorant and afraid, and I hoped that I could have the same power in the field as I had had in my classroom: I ask, others answer. While on Walpole Island, I was hoping to have the self-assurance that other researchers seemed to have—researchers whose interpretations were guided by conceptual frameworks that defined the possible ways of knowing.

---

1. I thank Marlene Sawatsky for this point.

I was pretty certain that I would find proof that indigenous Walpole Island traditions supported the social movement theories that I advocated. However, I was not comfortable with my desire to hide behind the regime of truth I had available to me as a nearly accredited professor; rather, I wanted to conduct what I now understand to be "empowering research": inquiry "on," "for," and "with" the people being researched. In other words, I wanted to engage in advocacy—to be committed to the subject's position.

More significant than biases themselves are the way that they are affected by participant-observation. In the end, participant observations demand that the researcher shed her/his taken-for-granted assumptions. To rest in the taken-for-granted eschews a critical stance and allows one to find comfort and meaning in practices whose premises remain undisclosed. Critical thinking, on the other hand, entails problematizing the assumed and accepted, and this requires acknowledging that the world in which we live is socially constructed and that the "truth" that it provides is provisional. Critical thinking also entails accepting responsibility for our own roles in the research process. Thus participant-observation assists the researcher in being more honest while advocating the individual's social identity by revealing its relationship to local culture. In other words, the social scientist—equal parts theorist and advocate—contributes to the personal empowerment of the people she/he researches. And I firmly believe that my main theoretical point, which is implied in all that I deal with in this book, is of the utmost significance to Walpole Island and other First Nations: The harm that corporate practices cause must be documented in terms of cultural devastation as well as in terms of actual physical devastation.

THEORY

Touraine (1985, 777; 1988, 129) is credited with suggesting that the analytical possibilities of grassroots activism may be extended by examining them in terms of new social movement theory. Such a step necessitates looking at the "particular historical conjuncture" pertinent to what one is examining. I take this to mean that not only should critical approaches to social movements integrate the idea of modernity and the notion of the subject, but also that the individual and his or her motives should be conceptualized against the backdrop of the type of society concerned—who has the power, how it is transferred, and why it is interspersed in the way that it is. This ensures that social movement theory looks at the social interactions that pattern power relations and at how, in turn, these are inscribed in, for example, employment possibilities, life chances, and the environment.

I found that the power relations that held the most significance for Walpole Islanders had to do with how modernity causes breaks with the past—breaks that have jeopardized the adhesive quality of the community. The threat brought on by these breaks has resulted in a cultural resurgence that has intensified the power of residents to resist unwanted social pressures. The question is, what has environmental threat got to do with the recognition that modern society is bringing to the fore environmentally destructive power relations?

For Walpole, modernity has meant both the loss of Nature and the loss of consciousness of that loss—a double-barreled blow that increases the distance between human and the non-human world (Rogers 1994). The cause: considering Nature in cost-benefit terms; that is, as a resource rather than as a process. The relations between industrial society and Nature have to be examined carefully; ideas and ideologies that contribute to seeing Nature as a resource (management, sustainability, quotas, stocks) have to be interrogated. Humans are complicit in capital's exploitation of nature, distorting the ideas and values (such as those of the Walpole Island community) that do not treat our particular economic stage as rational and inevitable. How do we reduce this distortion?

As Taylor and Whittier (1992, 109–110) explain, "collective actors do not exist de facto by virtue of individuals sharing a common structural location; they are created in the course of social movement activity." This does not mean that daily rallies or protests are necessary. In closing the distance between researcher and researched (in this case, those engaged in collective protest) one feels personal and collective identities being reshaped, notions of fairness and justice being redefined, community consensus being assembled, and solidarity being fostered. Bracketing my experience as a participant would no doubt leave me without the tools to relate to the cultivation of collective ideologies, the adjudication of group boundaries, the collectively negotiated meanings, and the development of an oppositional consciousness. What is more, it lets slip the chance for an interaction that fosters collective action.

As I mentioned in Chapter 6, a middle-aged woman from Walpole Island once explained to me that humans are parasites feeding off their host, the natural world, without acknowledging any connection to it. My immediate thought was that she was lamenting the fact that there is an almost complete ignorance of what Serres calls the Natural Contract—celebrations of such natural offerings of the movement of clouds and ripples. Later, I thought she was saying that it was due to our ignorance that we thought we had the right to feed off others. Perhaps, I thought, our willingness to take advantage of others starts during our stay in the womb, where we feed off the nourishment that our mothers give us. Indeed, this right might even gather energy during infancy when it defines our relationship with our parents—perhaps becoming a metaphor when, as mature members of industrialized nations, we are complicit in the ontological argument that grounds capital enterprises. As I wrote and re-wrote this experience, I came to the realization that this woman's analogy was a cautionary tale.

I now understand that her image of the parasite was meant to warn me not to nurture my ambitions or exorcise my guilt on the "case" of Walpole Island. Perhaps she knew from the questions I was asking that, in trying to make sense of identity, ethnicity, and race, I was occasionally inclined to acquiesce to essentialist notions—ideas that might predispose me to acclaiming First Nations as potential environmental messiahs. I think she also had a more modest goal in mind: she wanted me to see that we don't need to be parasites—that we don't need to mortgage future prosperity for the sake of contemporary "asocial" views of the environment.

Building on what others think (cf. Bash 1995; Johnston and Klandermans 1995; Swidler 1986), my findings suggest that subjective interpretations—both hers and mine—are not just crucial to the construction of social "problems" and, hence, to the mobilization requisite to addressing those problems. The notion of meaning construction has the ability to illuminate the links that lead to the individual's decision to engage in collective action. In other words, collective action frames are bridged, elaborated, extended, and transformed in a contentious dialectic between the SMO's framing practices and the individual experiences, meanings, and values embedded in culture. This is why exploring meaning construction has the potential to tell us something about the adherence of social movements across diverse cultural circumstances. Social movements are embedded in the community; the emergence of any social movement involves the constant push and pull of constituent values that are drawn from the culture(s) in question. These values are given meaning when compared to other ways of living and thinking. This comparison illuminates differences between alternatives and so allows for the emergence of a movement ideology that affirms counterhegemonic cultural practices (i.e., protest). Comparisons also establish what is seen to be an "objective" set of circumstances, which act as a major impetus for the SMO's official ideology, and influence a variety of individual experiences and social conditions which, in turn, mold the individual constituent and the collective constituency (Gamson 1992; Klandermans 1992).

Theorists have suggested the importance of meaning construction with regard to frame alignment and the mobilization of SMO recruits (cf. Johnston and Klandermans 1995; Klandermans 1992; Larana et al. 1994; Klandermans et al. 1988; Morris and McClurg-Mueller 1992). These theorists concentrate on the relationship between SMO and culture as the point of departure for (1) analyzing meaning construction and (2) critiquing the insufficient consideration that has been given to SMOs as producers of meaning. In other words, approaches to social movement theory that do not heed Touraine's call for incorporating motives into their analyses do not adequately document the fact that individuals construct meanings around the SMOs of the world and so determine the collective action frame that they adopt. In other words, local culture is an essential part of any social movement.

Local culture is a community's enduring expressive elements and its patterns of meanings; it is made up of the political thoughts, feelings, and behavior of its members. These cultural items are the fabric of community life and bring into being the empirical thrust of any given social movement. The threat of environmental destruction on Walpole Island was interpreted by Islanders as an attack on their community. And while it is the community's cultural traditions that have formed the basis of its response to this attack, it is the ceaseless individual interactions that are responsible for those traditions. As Sztompka (1991, 156) explains, "social movements embody the characteristic two-sidedness of social reality, the dialectics of individuals and social wholes." The recursive work of social movements is made possible because these movements have "a mediating location between the preexistent structure, out of which the movement itself emerges, and the later structure, modified under its impact" (Sztompka 1991, 156). In others words, Sztompka stresses the need for social movement theory to recognize the relationship between individual action and collective action frames (as prefigured in the culture of the community in question). Seen in this way, social movements are

> forms of cognitive praxis which are shaped by both external and internal political processes. Social movements express shifts in the consciousness of actors as they are articulated in the interactions between activists and their opposition(s) in historically situated political and cultural contexts. The content of this consciousness, what we call the cognitive praxis of a movement, is socially conditioned, it depends upon the conceptualization of a problem which is bound by the concerns of historically situated actors and on the reactions of their opponents. (Eyerman and Jamison 1991, 4)

The message is that frame alignment occurs when the individual agrees to partisan status. The possibility of that status occurs at the point where collective action frame meets individual meanings and both are congruent with the problem defined by the SMO. The individual is engaged in constructing meaning and, thus, in processing the experiences, values, beliefs, and practices that constitute culture. Social movement theorists need to broaden their scope in order to incorporate the rather obvious fact that the individual's meaning formation is infused by culture—by community meanings that reflect the local character of what people do, where they live, and the power they do or do not have.

This book confirms these observations. The Heritage Centre has recognized that its framing activity must represent Anishinabe culture. As such, the Heritage Centre is a voice for the community, allowing Anishinabe values and beliefs to be solidified and then disseminated to others. Frames are representations of the Anishinabe, or Walpole Island, culture that have been mediated by the Heritage Centre for non-Native consumption. Furthermore, the overarching function of the collective action frame is to communicate a meta-message in terms that will engage outside sympathy. It illuminates the role of particular aspects of culture in a community-based movement. This was demonstrated by the continued expansion of the ecological Native/sustainable community collective action frame, which eventually spoke to the protection of Walpole Island's natural heritage in a way that resonated with mainstream values and beliefs. The expansion of the collective action frame increases the level of congruence between the beliefs of the Heritage Centre and its potential constituency while cultivating the niche in the mainstream imagination reserved for the "indigenous environmentalist."

CONSCIOUSNESS, COLLECTIVE IDENTITY, AND SOLIDARITY REVISITED

The concept of consciousness as it has been detailed in the social movement literature captures the move from grievance to protest. For example, Klandermans (1992, 78) takes the position that "collective action proceeds from a significant transformation in the collective consciousness of the actors involved." Tarrow (1991, 414) expands upon Klandermans's position, judging consciousness to be a "distinct analytical stage in the process of decisions to participate in social movement activity." These theorists stress the ability of constituents to reproduce, contest, and rebuild social relations based upon the dissemination of knowledge. According to Eyerman and Jamison (1991, 164): "What earlier critical theorists called consciousness is not an individual possession, determined by structural relationships, but a form of identity, a kind of knowledge that is formed in the context of a social movement."

Gamson (1992, 67), for one, agrees with Eyerman and Jamison conceptualizing the relationship between consciousness and identity "as the interplay between two levels—between individuals who operate actively in the construction of meanings and socio-cultural processes that offer meanings." I agree with these two assessments: consciousness is infused by specific values and beliefs that correspond with the willingness of individuals to engage in collective action once they have interpreted their objective conditions as being intolerable. This follows Taylor and Whittier's (1992, 114) description of consciousness as the existence of "interpretive frameworks that emerge from a group's struggle to define and realize members' common interests in opposition to the dominant order."

With regard to Walpole Island, the role of culture in consciousness is seen in the invocation of a Native identity. Partially pan-Native in origin, this identity was augmented by a particular set of Anishnabe responsibilities. For example, the Women of

Bkejwanong are responsible for the health of the water. On Walpole Island, collective identity is rooted in defining certain situations as unjust and collectively transferring the consequent feeling of grievance into demands. Some researchers have suggested that the process of moving from consciousness to collective identity is at the root of social movement formation (McAdam 1982; Feree and Miller 1985). I would extend this understanding of the relationship between consciousness and collective identity. Consciousness involves (1) defining the roots of a problem, (2) suggesting collective rather than individual solutions to it, and (3) identifying antagonists.

If, as Taylor and Whittier assert, social mobilization relies upon the "shared definitions of a group that derives from members' common interests, experiences, and solidarity" (1992, 105), then collective identity can be analyzed in terms of how it fosters solidarity. In fact, shared definitions do add to the typical meanings attached to collective identity. In its emphasis on reciprocal networks of exchange, collective identity not only details the emergence of a social movement constituency, but also a high degree of self-understanding. Shared definitions result in solidarity and bring together the individual and the community. The overlap between the individual and the community leads to the expression of shared meanings as oppositional practices. Maintaining this community-based social movement then, requires planning and organization, necessitating what Stoecker (1994, 226) calls solidarity, or a "group of people who share a common culture and care of one another." How is it possible to conclude this?

On Walpole Island there is an ancient Native cultural framework. This framework is important to the Walpole Island population, whose values and beliefs have their roots in what residents refer to as "time immemorial," "the beginning of time," and so on. The community's relationship to the non-human environment is tied to an identity that involves the former protecting the latter. How community members view environmental degradation is based on traditional cultural beliefs, and community consciousness emerges and is strengthened by its links to collective identity. On Walpole Island this identity is encapsulated by particular moments in time—moments that reinforce the relationship between the human and non-human worlds. The resulting "we-ness" is articulated around an emerging awareness of community expertise and the potential for translating this knowledge into a model for outside action and instruction. In other words, the Heritage Centre is trying to make use of values and beliefs that suggest both a traditional and contemporary "social contract" with nature.

It would appear reasonable to conclude that the utility of the environmental justice framework for Native communities lies in its privileging the way in which Native communities look at human social relations with the non-human world. In other words, enlarging the environmental justice discourse by incorporating Native activism becomes possible once one takes local culture seriously. The Walpole Island community represents a living argument for the fact that we simply cannot alter our environment with impunity. As de Certeau (1986, 231) explains, the fact that Walpole Island maintains a local culture is important but not surprising.

> At a time when the idea and effectiveness of Western democracy are everywhere undermined by the expansion of cultural and economic technocracy, and are in the process of slowly disintegrating along with what had been that system's condition of possibility (differences between local units and the autonomy of their sociopolitical representations); at a time when micro-experiments and explorations in self-management are attempting to compensate for the evolution toward centralization by recreating the diversity of local democracies—it is the same Indian communities which were oppressed and eclipsed by the Western "democracies" that are now proving to be the only ones capable of offering modes of self-management based on a multi-centennial history.

Fortunately, I think, the residents of Walpole Island are increasingly receptive to the burden of acknowledging their ability to reflect on the environmental repercussions of all human activities. What is more redeeming, though, is the revelation of a self-conscious, self-reflective community engaged in a long-term and continuing process of tempering the impact of uninvited and unwanted outside influences. This community's potential mobilization around the environmental justice framework offers a context for recognizing the alternately malleable and immutable character of identity. Specifically, in a time when the undisputed exclusion of nature from culture is being questioned as a cultural premise, the community of Walpole Island stands out as an example of what can be accomplished through the power of a collective identity.

SOME FINAL WORDS: ALTERNATIVES

I recommend that environmental justice advocates[2] use Walpole Island as a model for philosophical, spiritual, and communal organization. I suggest creating an independent environmental justice institute on Walpole Island. This idea emerged in conversations with community members, who want a wilderness camp for youth and/or an outdoor education center. One middle-aged interviewee, named Stella, saw the need for a wilderness camp, as she believed that real teaching and learning have been absent since people entered institutionalized classrooms. Furthermore, the Heritage Centre's practice of taking strangers through the wetlands for a brief visit always produces greater understanding and sympathy for the community's plight. And my own experience of living in the community was integral to my understanding of environmental justice and its relationship to Walpole Island culture. Accordingly, I would encourage those interested in similar issues to engage in similar experiences.

I believe that Walpole Islanders embody a history and a tradition of environmental concern. Moreover, as an undertaking, this projected environmental justice institute would be capable of growing and adapting new ways of thinking and responding to various issues and intellectual projects. I also believe that the creation of this learning institute would lead to a reduction in the numbers of external auditors and other environmental specialists who have felt the need to drop in and assess the community, with seemingly little regard for how it is affected by environmental issues. I suggest that Walpole Island host a number of visitors each year and that these visitors learn by residing in the community

---

2. This section's specific audience is Walpole Island residents, but I am also hopeful that environmentalists may look at it and re-evaluate practices that perpetuate the ecological Native stereotype. This stereotype is the product of a Euro-Canadian culture, and I am suggesting what I refer to as AlterNatives (a one-week symposium to be hosted at the Walpole Island First Nation Institute for the Study of Environmental Justice) as a way to, among other things, unlearn this type of discrimination.

while taking part in a one-week symposium. This one-week symposium might be called "AlterNatives," and it could be hosted at the Walpole Island First Nation Institute for the Study of Environmental Justice.

AlterNatives could offer knowledge based on mainstream science and technology (such as air monitoring, soil testing, and toxicology). It could ensure that the community is able to share its story and, therefore, add traditional knowledge to scientific knowledge. Elders, hunters, and guides could be brought in to explain the community; visitors could be taken through the marshes, the oak savannas, or Tahgoning enterprises. The people of Walpole are knowledgeable and approachable, and they know so much about "their community."

AlterNatives would offer activist training directed by actual issues in the Walpole Island struggle. Walpole Island is a perfect location for studying environmental issues that have been taken up at the local community level. Strategies and tactics employed, such as anti-spill marches, could be augmented or examined for flaws. AlterNatives would be an excellent place at which to begin discussing the level of influence of contemporary culture on community identity, and it would allow for some very "newsworthy" press.

AlterNatives could supply internships or apprenticeships for residents. Besides the obvious experience such internships would supply, these "field symposia" would reinforce respect for, and a harmonious relationship with, the environment as part of this community's value system. AlterNatives would be a community model for youth. In addition, local artists, writers, and activists could infuse the center with a variety of data.

The field symposia could work to integrate visitors into the community movement, as it is likely that the one-week stay would result in their being very concerned about Walpole Island's plight. There could be a reciprocal arrangement whereby, in exchange for the Walpole Island story, visitors could offer ideas about developing tools to fight pollution. Visitors could be induced to participate in a structured grassroots event, such as witnessing the continued existence of unsustainable practices.

AlterNatives could be a site for fostering and controlling relationships with academics, academic institutions, and governments. Walpole Islanders could inform the environmental movement of what it needs to do to attract a broad base of support. This would include (1) articulating the traditional relationship between Native people and their natural surroundings; (2) recounting how colonialist views of Native people led to the exploitation and destruction of this "resource"; and (3) assessing damage occurring to both the human and non-human environment.

NATIVE ENVIRONMENTAL JUSTICE FRAMEWORK

I also propose developing a strategic framework dedicated to recognizing and resolving Native-Canadian environmental justice concerns. Environmental justice considers environmental issues within their social contexts. The central argument is that the private control of production has fostered circumstances within which race, class, and gender are determining factors with regard to who experiences a disproportionate amount of environmental risk. Parties adopting an environmental justice stance support the principles of the environmental justice movement, which can be summarized as the right to have access to information on risk, the right to see the equal weighting of claims, the right to fair compensation, and the right to have an equal voice in the decision-making process. Therefore, I suggest that the empirical thrust of environmental justice research combine the identification of data sources, the analysis of community impacts, the identification of at-risk and vulnerable populations, and the assessment of disproportionate impacts.

In order to produce a strategic Native environmental justice framework, I would suggest developing a theoretical orientation that brings together postcolonial thought, environmental justice, and First Nations studies. This perspective would be grounded in a systematic examination and classification of databases, journals, government documents, and First Nations communities according to three analytical categories. The first category would be the traditional relationship between Native peoples and their natural surroundings, the second would be Native views of postcolonial forces, and the third would be the damage occurring to both the human and non-human environment in Native communities.

Describing and analyzing environmental justice issues according to these categories would create comparative analytical structures that could establish links between First Nations and other people concerned with the use and occupation of the environment. These links could be highlighted to facilitate knowledge and understanding, and, in so doing, they could reshape a number of different but not incompatible points of view. I also think that this framework could cultivate points of intersection prior to the convening of a negotiation between First Nations and second parties, thus facilitating a quick and productive start to substantive negotiations. Finally, this framework could allow for establishing "teaching beyond the classroom" as an ongoing research project. In collaboration with instructors, students could research environmental justice issues. This would allow for coordinating student research on social issues in response to specific questions and concerns posed by community groups, public-interest organizations, and local governments. Done in the context of course work, this could encourage and support the transfer and sharing of indigenous knowledge.

References

Adair, Margo and Sharon Howell. 1990. "Embracing Diversity." *Environmental Action*. January/February: 28.

Agar, Michael. 1986. *Speaking of Ethnography. Qualitative Research Method Series #2*. Newbury Park, California: Sage.

"Air-Monitoring Station at St. Anne's." 1988, 22 January. *Jibkenyan*. 2.

"Air-Testing Station Operating." 1988, 29 January. *Chatham Daily News*. 14.

Almeida, Paul. 1994. "The Network for Environmental and Economic Justice in the Southwest: Interview with Richard Moore." *Capitalism, Nature and Socialism* 5: 21–54.

"Animal Analysis." 1985, 15 March. *Jibkenyan*. 3.

"Another Spill!" 1991, 11 January. *Jibkenyan*. 3.

"Approximately 50 Attended the Mother's Day Environmental Rally in Sarnia." 1991, 17 May. *Jibkenyan*. 3.

Aronowitz, Stanley. 1992. *The Politics of Identity: Class, Culture, and Social Movements*. New York: Routledge.

Atkins, Thomas. 1990. "Living Up To Responsibilities." *Environmental Action*. January/February: 29–30.

Austin, Regina and Michael Schill. 1994. "Black, Brown, Red, and Poisoned." Pp. 53–74 in *Unequal Protection: Environmental Justice and Communities of Color*, edited by Robert Bullard. San Francisco: Sierra Club Books.

Bammer, Gabriele and Brian Martin. 1992. "Repetition Strain Injury in Australia: Medical Knowledge, Social Movement, and De Facto Partisanship." *Social Problems* 39: 219–237.

"Band Wants More Data Before Pipeline Decision." 1992, 14 May. *London Free Press*. 5.

Bash, Harry H. 1994. "Social Movements and Social Problems: Toward a Conceptual Rapprochement." Pp. 247–284 in *Research in Social Movements, Conflicts and Change*, edited by Louis Kriesberg, Michael Dobkowski, and Isidor Walliman. Greenwich, Connecticut: JAI Press.

Bash, Harry H. 1995. *Social Problems and Social Movements: An Exploration into the Sociological Construction of Alternative Realities.* Newark, N.J.: Humanities Press.

Benford, Robert. 1994. "Social Movements." Pp. 1880–1887 in *Encyclopedia of Sociology,* edited by Edgar F. and Marie L. Borgatta. New York: Macmillan.

Benton-Banai, Eddie. 1988. *The Mishomis Book: The Voice of the Ojibway.* Madison: Red School House.

Berry, John. 1992. *Health: Psychological Impacts.* A Report Prepared for the Moose River/James Bay Coalition during the Ontario Hydro Demand/Supply Hearings.

Best, Joel. 1989. *Images of Issues: Typifying Contemporary Social Problems.* New York: Aldine de Gruyter.

Best, Joel. 1993. "But Seriously Folks: The Limitations of the Strict Constructionist Interpretation of Social Problems." Pp. 109–127 in *Constructionist Controversies: Issues in Social Problems Theory,* edited by Gale Miller and James A. Holstein. New York: Aldine de Gruyter.

"Billions of Gallons of Toxic Waste May Be Leaking into River: Official." 1985, 29 November. *Jibkenyan.* 1.

"The 'Blob' One Year Later: Tip of a Pollution Iceberg." 1986, 17 September. *Jibkenyan.* 1.

Blumer, Herbert. 1939. "Collective Behavior." Pp. 65–121 in *Principles of Sociology,* edited by Alfred McClung Lee. New York: Barnes and Noble.

Bohanan, Paul. 1995. *How Culture Works.* New York: Free Press.

Bolsenga, Stanley J. and Maxwell Herdendorf. 1993. *Lake Erie and Lake St. Clair Handbook.* Detroit: Wayne State University Press.

Brown, Lester R., ed. 1991. *The World Watch Reader on Global Environmental Issues.* New York: W. W. Norton & Company.

Bryant, Bunyon, ed. 1995. *Environmental Justice: Issues, Policies and Struggles.* Washington D.C.: Island Press.

Bryant, Pat. 1990. "A Lily-White Achilles Heel." *Environmental Action.* January/February: 28–29.

Buege, Douglas, J. 1996. "The Ecologically Noble Savage Revisited." *Environmental Ethics* 18 (Spring): 71–88.

Bullard, Robert D. 1990. *Dumping in Dixie: Race, Class, and Environmental Quality.* Boulder, Colorado: Westview Press.

Bullard, Robert D. 1992. *Confronting Environmental Racism: Voices from the Grassroots.* Boston: South End Press.

Bullard, Robert D., ed. 1994. *Unequal Protection: Environmental Justice and Communities of Color.* San Francisco: Sierra Club Books.

Cable, Sherry and Michael Benson. 1993. "Acting Locally: Environmental Injustice and the Emergence of Grass-roots Environmental Organizations." *Social Problems* 40: 464–477.

"Care Needed in Water Situation." 1985, 16 October. *Wallaceburg News.* 2.

"CCCW Questions MOE Spokesman." 1986, 8 January. *Wallaceburg News.* 3.

Certeau, Michel de. 1986. *Heterologies: Discourse on the Other.* Minneapolis: University of Minnesota Press.

Chehak, Gail E. and Suzan Shown Harjo. 1990. "Protection Quandary in Indian Country." *Environmental Action.* January/February: 21–22.

"Chemical Spill—Again!!" 1994, 18 February. *Jibkenyan.* 1.

"Chief Demands Emergency Task-Force on Environment." 1991, 26 July. *Jibkenyan.* 1.

"Chief Expresses Environmental Concerns." 1990, 24 August. *Jibkenyan.* 4.

Chreod Environmental Consultants. 1993. *Environmental Audit of the Walpole Island First Nation.*

Churchill, Ward. 1992. *Struggle for the Land: Indigenous Resistance to Genocide, Ecocide, and Contemporary North America.* Toronto: Between the Lines.

Churchill, Ward. 1993. *Indians Are Us? Culture and Genocide in Native North America.* Toronto: Between the Lines.

"Civil Disobedience Planned by Citizen's Group." 1986, 5 Febuary. *Wallaceburg News.* 5.

"Clean Water War Brewing on Walpole." 1994, 10 February. *Chatham Daily News.* 1.

"Coalition Disputes Ministry's Conclusions." 1986, 8 January. *Wallaceburg Courier Press.* 8.

Cohen, Jean L. 1985. "Strategy or Identity: New Theoretical Paradigms and Contemporary Social Movements." *Social Research* 52: 663–716.

"Conservation Club off to Good Start." 1988, 29 April. *Jibkenyan.* 4.

"Conservation Club Up-Date." 1994, 8 July. *Jibkenyan.* 7.

"Continued Spills Anger Walpole's Isaac." 1994, 8 February. *Chatham Daily News.* 4.

Cormack, Michael. 1992. *Ideology.* Ann Arbor: University of Michigan Press.

Couch, Carl. 1968. "Collective Behaviour: An Examination of Some Stereotypes." *Social Problems* 15: 310–322.

Couple Concerned about Wallaceburg Water. 1990, 25 August. *Chatham Daily News.* 16.

Couture, Joseph E. 1996. "The Role of Native Elders: Emergent Issues." Pp. 41–56 in *Visions of the Heart: Canadian Aboriginal Issues,* edited by David Alan Long and Olive Patricia Dickinson. Toronto: Harcourt Brace.

"Crimes Against Mother Earth: An Environmental Hearing." 1991, 19 April. *Jibkenyan.* 3.

Dalton, Russel J., Manfred Keuchler, and Wilhelm Burklin. 1990. "The Challenge of New Movements." Pp. 3–16 in *Challenging the Political Order: New Social and Political Movements in Western Democracies,* edited by Russel J. Dalton and Manfred Kuechler. New York: Oxford University Press.

Danahy, Jennifer. 1996. "An Archeology of Environmental Injustice: Walpole Island, Ontario." Unpublished paper in Faculty of Environmental Studies. York University.

Darnovsky, Marcy. 1992. "Stories Less Told: Histories of US Environmentalism." *Socialist Review* 21: 11–54.

Davies, Katherine and Margaret A. Wheatley. 1994. "Bkejwanong: Our Environment, Our Health." *Effects on Aboriginals from the Great Lakes Environment Interim Report.* An Assembly of First Nations–Health Canada Partnership.

Denzin, Norman K. 1989a. *Interpretive Biography.* Newbury Park, California: Sage.

Denzin, Norman K. 1989b. *The Research Act: A Theoretical Introduction to Sociological Methods.* Englewood Cliffs, N.J.: Prentice-Hall.

Di Chiro, Giovanna. 1992. "Defining Environmental Justice: Women's Voices and Grassroots Politics." *Socialist Review* 21: 93–130.

"Dioxin Has Been in River 10 Years, Official Says." 1988, 4 November. *Toronto Star.* 4.

"Divers in River Find Another Festering Blob." 1995, 8 December. *Jibkenyan.* 2.

"Dow and Walpole Still at Odds." 1992, 15 January. *London Free Press.* 13.

"Dow Appearance at 'Burg Council Sparks Debate." 1986, 19 November. *Chatham Daily News.* 12.

"Dow Still Trucking Water to Walpole." 1994, 9 February. *London Free Press.* 8.

"Dow, Walpole Officials to Discuss Spills Monday." 1994, 12 February. *London Free Press.* 11.

Dowie, Ian. 1995. *Losing Ground: American Environmentalism at the Close of the Twentieth Century.* Cambridge, Massachusetts: MIT Press.

"Drinking Water Trucked in for Residents." 1985, 15 November. *Jibken-yan.* 1.

Dyck, Noel and James B. Waldram, eds. 1993. *Anthropology, Public Policy, and Native Peoples in Canada.* Montreal/Kingston: McGill-Queen's University Press.

"The EAGLE Project Hopes to Help Make the Great Lakes Great Again." 1993, 5 March. *Jibkenyan.* 5.

"Eating Patterns Survey." 1993, 15 October. *Jibkenyan.* 11.

Eder, Klaus. 1985. "The 'New Social Movements': Moral Crusades, Political Pressure Groups, or Social Movements." *Social Research* 52: 869–890.

Effects on Aboriginals from the Great Lakes Environment Project (1993–94). Annual Report. An Assembly of First Nations–Health Canada Partnership.

"Eloquent Island Speaks to Environment Minister." 1992, 22 May. *Walla-ceburg News.* 6.

Engle, Claude. 1990. "Profiles: Environmental Action in Minority Communities." *Environmental Action.* January/February: 22–25.

"Environment Is #1 Concern." 1989, 29 September. *Jibkenyan.* 2.

"Environmental Concerns." 1989, 26 May. *Jibkenyan.* 2.

"Environmental Notes." 1991, 8 March. *Jibkenyan.* 5.

"Environmental Notes." 1993, 25 June. *Jibkenyan.* 5.

"Environmental Notes." 1996, 13 May. *Jibkenyan.* 6.

"Environmental/Pollution Concerns, a #1 Priority for Island Members." 1988, 22 July. *Jibkenyan.* 1.

"Environmental Research and Protection: Vitally Important for Future Generations." 1983, 16 December. *Jibkenyan.* 4.

Evernden, Neil. 1989. "Nature in Industrial Society." Pp. 65–81 in *Cultural Politics in Contemporary America,* edited by Ian Angus and Sut Jhally. New York: Routledge.

"Expectant Mothers Concerned about Effects of C.I.L.'s Recent Spill." 1989, 31 March. *Jibkenyan.* 2.

Eyerman, Ron and Andrew Jamison. 1991. *Social Movements: A Cognitive Approach.* University Park, Pennsylvania: The Pennsylvania University Press.

Fantasia, Rick. 1988. *Cultures of Solidarity: Consciousness, Action, and Contemporary American Workers.* Berkeley: University of California Press.

"Fears Grow over St. Clair Pollution." 1985, September 25. *Chatham Daily News.* 4.

Featherstone, Mike. 1991. *Consumer Culture and the Postmodernism.* London: Sage.

Feilding, Robert and Anne S. Feilding. 1986. *Linking Data. Qualitative Research Method Series #4.* Beverly Hills, California: Sage.

Feree, Myra Marx. 1992. "Political Context of Rationality: Rational Choice Theory and Resource Mobilization." Pp. 53–76 in *Frontiers in Social Movement Theory,* edited by Aldon D. Morris and Carol McClurg Mueller. New Haven, Connecticut: Yale University Press.

Feree, Myra Marx and Frederick D. Miller. 1985. "Mobilization and Meaning: Toward an Integration of Social Psychology and Resource Mobilization Perspectives on Social Movements." *Sociological Inquiry* 55: 38–61.

"First Nation, Dow Declare Truce in Water War." 1994, 15 February. *Chatham Daily News.* 5.

Fitzsimmons-Lecavalier, Patricia and Guy Lecavalier. 1986. "Social Movements and Social Change." Pp. 556–586 in *Sociology,* edited by Robert Hagedorn. Toronto: Holt, Rinehart and Winston.

Fontaine, Jerry et al. 1997. "Resource and Environmental Issues," Pp. 168–191 in *Aboriginal Issues Today: A Legal and Business Guide,* edited by Stephen B. Smart and Michael Coyle. North Vancouver, BC: Self-Counsel Press.

Fox, Glen. 1991. "International Joint Commission Workshop on Cause-Effect Linkages." *Journal of Toxicology and Environmental Health* 3: v–x.

Fox, Glen. 1994. "Scientific Principles." Pp. 2–5 in *Applying Weight of Evidence: Issues and Practice,* edited by Michael Gilbertson and Sally Cole-Misch. Windsor, Ontario: International Joint Commission.

Francis, Daniel. 1992. *The Imaginary Indian: The Image of the Indian in Canadian Culture.* Vancouver: Arsenal Pulp Press.

Freeman, Jo. 1975. *The Politics of Women's Liberation.* New York: David McKay.

Freeman, Jo. 1983a. "A Model for Analyzing the Strategic Options of Social Movement Organizations." Pp. 193–210 in *Social Movements of the Sixties and Seventies,* edited by Jo Freeman. New York: Longman.

Freeman, Jo. 1983b. "On the Origins of Social Movements." Pp. 8–32 in *Social Movements of the Sixties and Seventies,* edited by Jo Freeman. New York: Longman.

Friedman, Debra and Doug McAdam. 1992. "Collective Identity and Activism: Networks, Choices, and the Life of a Social Movement." Pp. 77–96 in *Frontiers in Social Movement Theory,* edited by Aldon D. Morris and Carol McClurg Mueller. New Haven, Connecticut: Yale University Press.

"Fur Industry Collapses." 1990, 16 November. *Jibkenyan*. 5.

"Future of Walpole Linked to St. Clair River." 1991, 1 May. *Wallaceburg Courier Press*. 3.

Gamson, William A. 1975. *The Strategy of Social Protest*. Homewood, Illinois: Dorsey Press.

Gamson, William A. 1988. "Political Discourse and Collective Action." Pp. 219–246 in *From Structure to Action: Comparing Social Movement Research Across Cultures (International Social Movement Research 1)*, edited by Bert Klandermans, Hanspeter Kreisi, and Sidney Tarrow. Greenwich, Connecticut: JAI Press.

Gamson, William A. 1992. "The Social Psychology of Collective Action." Pp. 53–76 in *Frontiers in Social Movement Theory*, edited by Aldon D. Morris and Carol McClurg Mueller. New Haven, Connecticut: Yale University Press.

Gedicks, Al. 1993. *The New Resource Wars: Native and Environmental Struggles Against Multinational Corporations*. Boston: South End Press.

Geertz, Clifford. 1973. *The Interpretation of Cultures: Selected Essays by Clifford Geertz*. New York: BasicBooks.

Georges, Robert A. and Michael D. Jones. 1980. *People Studying People: The Human Element in Fieldwork*. Berkeley: University of California Press.

Gerlach, Luther P. and Virginia H. Hine. 1970. *People, Power, Change: Movements of Social Transformation*. New York: Bobbs-Merrill.

Gilbertson, Michael. 1985. "The Niagara Labyrinth—The Human Ecology of Producing Organochlorine Chemicals." *Canadian Journal of Fisheries and Aquatorial Science* 42: 1681–1692.

Gilbertson, Michael. 1992. "PCB and Dioxin Research and Implications for Fisheries Research and Resource Management" *Canadian Journal of Fish and Aquatorial Science* 49: 1078–1079.

Gilbertson, Michael and R. Stephen Schneider. 1993. "Preface to the Special Section on Cause-Effect Linkages. Causality: The Missing Link Between Science and Policy." *Journal of Great Lakes Research* 19: 720–721.

Gismondi, Michael and Mary Richardson. 1994. "Discourse and Power in Environmental Politics: Public Hearings on a Bleached Kraft Pulp Mill in Alberta, Canada." Pp. 137–162 in *Is Capitalism Sustainable: Political Economy and the Politics of Ecology*, edited by Martin O'Connor. New York: Guilford.

Glaser, Barney and Anselm Strauss. 1967. *The Discovery of Grounded Theory: Strategies for Qualitative Research*. Chicago: Aldine.

Goldberg, Mira. 1995. "Toward Stronger Alliances: A Response to Re-thinking Environmental-First Nations Relationships." *Earth First!* April: 1–3.

Goldtooth, Tom. 1995 "Indigenous Nations: Summary of Sovereignty and Its Implications for Environmental Protection." Pp. 138–148 in *Environmental Justice: Issues, Policies and Struggles,* edited by Bunyon Bryant. Washington, D.C.: Island Press.

Good, E. Reginald. 1995. "Mississauga-Mennonite Relations in the Upper Grand River Valley." *Ontario History* 87: 155–172.

Goode, Erich. 1992. *Collective Behavior.* New York: Harcourt Brace Jovanovich.

Gottlieb, Robert. 1993. *Forcing the Spring: The Transformation of the American Environmental Movement.* Washington, D.C.: Island Press.

Great Lakes Science Advisory Board. 1993. *Report to the International Joint Commission.* Windsor, Ontario: International Joint Commission.

"Greenpeace Favours MOE Resignation." 1985, 7 November. *Chatham Daily News.* 11.

"Grier to Ink Treaties on Walpole Island Today." 1992, 21 May. *Chatham Daily News.* 7.

"Grier Visits Walpole, not Wallaceburg." 1992, 2 December. *Wallaceburg Courier Press.* 2.

Grow Richard. 1990. "Grammar for Ecologists." *Environmental Action.* January/February: 26.

Gusfield, Joseph. 1981. *The Culture of Public Problems.* Chicago: University of Chicago Press.

Gusfield, Joseph. 1989. "Constructing the Ownership of Social Problems: Fun and Profit in the Welfare State." *Social Problems* 36: 431–441.

Halberg, David. 1994. *The War Against the Greens.* San Francisco: Sierra Books.

Hale, Sylvia H. 1995. *Controversies in Sociology: A Canadian Introduction.* Mississauga, Ontario: Copp Clark.

Hannigan, John A. 1995. *Environmental Sociology: A Social Constructionist Perspective.* New York: Routledge.

Hanson, Jaydee. 1990. "Getting beyond C-ERA." *Environmental Action.* January/February: 27.

"Heath Effects Information Session." 1993, 3 September. *Jibkenyan.* 6.

Hedley, Max. 1986. "Community Based Research: The Dilemma of Contact." *Canadian Review of Sociology and Anthropology* 6: 91–103.

Hedley, Max. 1991. "Cooperative Intervention in a Reserve Context." Paper presented at the Centre for Welfare Studies. Wilfred Laurier University, October 3–5, 1991.

Higgins, Robert R. 1993. "Race and Environmental Equity: An Overview of the Environmental Justice Issue in the Policy Process." *Polity* 26: 281–300.

Hofrichter, Richard. 1993. *Toxic Struggles: The Theory and Practice of Environmental Justice.* Gabriola Island: New Society Publishers.

Hornborg, Alf. 1994. "Environmentalism, Ethnicity and Sacred Places: Reflections on Modernity, Discourse and Power." *Canadian Review of Sociology and Anthropology* 31(3): 245–267.

"How Much Is One Part per Billion?" 1986, 7 November. *Jibkenyan.* 4.

Hull, John and Michael C. Williams. 1992. "A Continuity of Tradition: A Place Where Native Americans Still Burn the Prairies and Oak Openings." *Restoration and Management Notes* 10: 38–39.

"Huron Pipeline Project: Walpole May Abandon Plan." 1992, 26 April. *Chatham Daily News.* 4.

Husserl, Edmund. 1970. *Crisis of European Sciences and Transcendental Phenomenology: An Introduction to Phenomenological Philosophy.* Evanston, Illinois: Northwestern University Press.

"ICI Seeks Permission to Dump." 1995, 17 May. *Chatham Daily News.* 1.

"Imprison Polluters, Walpole Chief Says." 1993, 14 May. *Jibkenyan.* 4.

"Input Being Sought on Area Wetlands." 1992, 7 January. *Chatham Daily News.* 13.

International Joint Commission. 1993. *A Strategy for Virtual Elimination of Persistent Toxic Substances: Report of the Virtual Elimination Task Force to the International Joint Commission (Volume 1).* Windsor, Ontario: International Joint Commission.

International Joint Commission. 1993. *A Strategy for Virtual Elimination of Persistent Toxic Substances: Seven Reports to the Virtual Elimination Task Force (Volume 2).* Windsor, Ontario: International Joint Commission.

Jacobs, Burton. 1990. "Kicking Out the Indian Agent on Walpole Island." *Anglican Magazine.* March: 27–29.

Jenkins, J. Craig. 1983. "The Transformation of a Constituency into a Movement: Farmworker Organizing in California." Pp. 52–70 in *Social Movements of the Sixties and Seventies,* edited by Jo Freeman. New York: Longman.

Johnston, Hank and Bert Klandermans, eds. 1995. *Social Movements and Culture* (Volume 4 of series entitled *Social Movements, Protest and Contention*). Minneapolis: University of Minnesota Press.

Kary, Alan. 1995. "Ideology, Identity and the Charter: Being Native in the 90's." Paper prepared for the New England Political Science Association Annual General Meeting. Portland, Maine, May 5–6.

Kitschelt, Herbert. 1991. "Resource Mobilization Theory: A Critique." Pp. 323–347 in *Research on Social Movements: The State of the Art in*

Western Europe and the USA, edited by Dieter Rucht. Boulder, Colorado: Westview Press.

Kitsuse, John I. and Malcolm Spector. 1973. "Toward a Sociology of Social Problems: Social Conditions, Value Judgements, and Social Problems." *Social Problems* 20: 407–419.

Klandermans, Bert. 1986. "New Social Movements and Resource Mobilization: The European and the American Approach." *International Journal of Mass Emergencies and Disasters* 4: 13–37.

Klandermans, Bert. 1988. "The Formation and Mobilization of Consensus." Pp. 173–196 in *From Structure to Action: Comparing Social Movement Research Across Cultures (International Social Movement Research 1),* edited by Bert Klandermans, Hanspeter Kreisi, and Sidney Tarrow. Greenwich, Connecticut: JAI Press.

Klandermans, Bert. 1992. "The Social Construction of Protest and Multiorganizational Fields." Pp. 53–76 in *Frontiers in Social Movement Theory,* edited by Aldon D. Morris and Carol McClurg Mueller. New Haven, Connecticut: Yale University Press.

Klandermans, Bert and Dirk Oegma. 1987. "Potential Networks, Motivations, and Barriers: Steps toward Participation in Social Movements." *American Sociological Review* 52: 519–531.

Klandermans, Bert and Sidney Tarrow. 1988. "Mobilization Into Social Movements: Synthesizing European and American Approaches." Pp. 1–40 in *From Structure to Action: Comparing Social Movement Research Across Cultures (International Social Movement Research 1),* edited by Bert Klandermans, Hanspeter Kreisi, and Sidney Tarrow. Greenwich, Connecticut: JAI Press.

Knox, Margaret. 1993. "Their Mother's Keeper." *Sierra.* May/June: 51–84.

Krauss, Celene. 1994. "Women of Color on the Front Line." Pp. 256–271 in *Unequal Protection: Environmental Justice and Communities of Color,* edited by Robert D. Bullard. San Francisco: Sierra Club Books.

Kuhn, Thomas S. 1970. *The Structure of Scientific Revolutions.* Chicago: University of Chicago Press.

LaDuke, Winona. 1992. "Preface" in *Struggle for the Land: Indigenous Resistance to Genocide, Ecocide, and Contemporary North America,* authored by Ward Churchill. Toronto: Between the Lines.

"Lake Huron Could Cost Millions—May Be Best Choice." 1987, 11 September. *Wallaceburg Courier Press.* 3.

"Lake Huron Pipeline Declared a Provincial Priority." 1987, 21 December. *Chatham Daily News.* 3.

Larana, Enrique, Hank Johnston, and Joseph R. Gusfield, eds. 1994. *New Social Movements: From Ideology to Identity.* Philadelphia: Temple University Press.

LeBon, Gustave. 1960. *The Crowd*. New York: Viking.

Lele, Jayant. 1995. *Hindutva: The Emergence of the Right*. Madras, India: Earthworm Books.

Li, Vivien, Winona LaDuke, Benjamin Chavis, Carl Anthony, Richard Moore, and Scott Douglas. 1993. "A Sierra Roundtable on Race, Justice, and Environment." *Sierra*. May/June: 51–58.

Lilliston, Ben. 1992. "Island of Poison." *Multinational Monitor*. September: 8–9.

"Local Officials Pleased with Outcome of Talks." 1985, 28 November. *Chatham Daily News*. 6.

Lofland, John. 1995. *Social Movement Organizations: Guide to Research on Insurgent Realities*. New York: Aldine de Gruyter.

Long, David. 1992. "Culture, Ideology and Militancy: The Movement of Indians in Canada 1969–1991." Pp. 118–134 in *Organizing Dissent: Contemporary Social Movements in Theory and Practice*, edited by William Carroll. Toronto: Garamond.

Mannheim, Karl. 1985. *Ideology and Utopia: An Introduction to the Sociology of Knowledge*. New York: Harcourt Brace Jovanovich.

Mauss, Armand. 1975. *Social Problems as Social Movements*. New York: J. B. Lippincott.

McAdam, Doug. 1982. *Political Process and the Development of Black Insurgency*. Chicago: University of Chicago Press.

McAdam, Doug. 1990. "Microstructural Bases of Recruitment to Social Movements." Pp. 1–34 in *Research in Social Movements: Conflict and Change*, edited by Louis Krieberg. Greenwich, Connecticut: JAI Press.

McCarthy, J. D. and M. N. Zald. 1973. *The Trend of Social Movements*. Morristown, N.J.: General Learning Press.

McClurg Mueller, Carol. 1992. "Building Social Movement Theory." Pp. 3–26 in *Frontiers in Social Movement Theory*, edited by Aldon D. Morris and Carol McClurg Mueller. New Haven, Connecticut: Yale University Press.

McPhail, Lee. 1991. *The Myth of the Madding Crowd*. New York: Aldine de Gruyter.

McQuarie, Donald. 1987. "The New Right and the Question of Ideological Hegemony." *The Psychohistory Review* 17: 109–142.

Melucci, Alberto. 1985. "The Symbolic Challenge of Contemporary Movements." *Social Research* 52: 781–816.

Melucci, Alberto. 1988. "Getting Involved: Identity and Mobilization in Social Movements." Pp. 329–348 in *From Structure to Action: Comparing Social Movement Research Across Cultures (International Social Movement Research 1)*, edited by Bert Klandermans, Hanspeter Kreisi, and Sidney Tarrow. Greenwich, Connecticut: JAI Press.

Melucci, Alberto. 1989. *Nomads of the Present: Social Movements and Individual Needs in Contemporary Society.* London: Hutchinson Radius.

Melucci, Alberto. 1992. "Liberation or Meaning? Social Movements, Culture and Democracy." *Development and Change* 23: 43–77.

Miles, Matthew and Michael A. Huberman. 1994. *Qualitative Data Analysis: A Sourcebook of New Methods.* Beverly Hills, California: Sage.

Miller, Gale and James A. Holstein. 1993. "Constructing Social Problems: Context and Legacy." Pp. 3–18 in *Constructionist Controversies: Issues in Social Problems Theory,* edited by Gale Miller and James A. Holstein. New York: Aldine de Gruyter.

Miller, Jim. 1993. *Aboriginal Conduct and Ethics.* Unpublished document.

Miller, Jim. 1995. *Chronology of Important Events on Walpole Island.* Unpublished document.

"Ministry's Credibility Questioned." 1986, 9 January. *Chatham Daily News.* 8.

Modavi, Neghin. 1991. "Environmentalism, State, and Economy in the United States." Pp. 261–273 in *Research in Social Movements, Conflicts and Change,* edited by Louis Kriesberg and Metta Spencer. Greenwich, Connecticut: JAI Press.

Morris, Aldon. 1984. *The Origins of the Civil Rights Movement.* New York: Free Press.

Morrison, James. 1994. "Upper Great Lakes Settlement: The Anishinabe–Jesuit Record" *Ontario History* 86: 53–71.

"Mother's Day Environmental Rally Being Planned...Participation Needed." 1991, 3 May. *Jibkenyan.* 1.

"Mutual 'Concerns' Accepted by Dow, Walpole." 1994, 15 February. *London Free Press.* 4.

Myers, Sheila, Jack Manno, and Kimberly McDade. 1995. "Great Lakes Human Health Effects Research in Canada and the United States: An Overview of Priorities and Issues." *Great Lakes Research Review* 1: 13–23.

Nagle, Joane. 1996. *American Indian Ethnic Renewal.* Philadelphia: Temple University Press.

Nahdee, Toni. 1991. *Final Report of Crimes Against Mother Earth: An Environmental Hearing.* Unpublished document from Walpole Island Heritage Centre.

"Natives Plan Protest of Valley Pollution." 1994, 26 April. *Sarnia News.* 4.

"Natives Seeking More Say on Environmental Bill of Rights Bill." 1992, 2 December. *Chatham Daily News.* 3.

"Natives Seeking Some Fast Answers." 1992, 2 December. *London Free Press*. 6.

"Natives Stage Rally Against Chemical Valley." 1994, 11 May. *Wallaceburg Courier Press*. 2.

"Natives Want Stop to Spills." 1993, 2 December. *London Free Press*. 6.

Neal, Arthur. 1970. "Conflict and the Functional Equivalence of Social Movements." *Sociological Focus* 3: 3–12

"New Citizens' Group Demands Clean Water." 1985, 27 November. *Wallaceburg News*. 1.

"New Meeting on Pipeline Ready to Go." 1988, 17 August. *Wallaceburg News*. 16.

"New Tests Show Local Water Safe." 1985, 22 November. *Wallaceburg News*. 1.

NIN.DA.WAAB.JIG. 1989. *Walpole Island: The Soul of Indian Territory*. Windsor, Ontario: Commercial Associates/Roy Ross.

Oberschall, Anthony. 1973. *Social Conflicts and Social Movements*. Englewood Cliffs, N.J.: Prentice-Hall.

Oberschall, Anthony. 1993. *Social Movements: Ideologies, Interests, and Identities*. New Brunswick, N.J.: Transaction Publishers.

Offe, Claus. 1985. "New Social Movements: Challenging the Boundaries of Institutional Politics." *Social Research* 52: 817–868.

"Oil Spill at Sarnia Puts 'Burg on Alert." 1988, 4 August. *Chatham Daily News*. 1.

Olson, Mancur. 1965. *The Logic of Collective Action*. Cambridge, Massachusetts: Harvard University Press.

"100 Marchers Protest St. Clair River Pollution." 1994, 9 May. *London Free Press*. 1.

"Our Environment Is #1 Issue, Says Chief." 1996, 13 October. *Jibkenyan*. 2.

Paishk, Emma. 1995. "A Residential School of Hurt and Rejection." *Jibkenyan*. October 13: 23.

Park, Robert and Ernest W. Burgess. 1931. *Introduction to the Science of Sociology*. Chicago: University of Chicago Press.

Pena, Milagros. 1992. "The Sodalititium Vitae Movement in Peru: A Rewriting of Liberation Theology." *Sociological Analysis* 53: 159–173.

Piven, Frances Fox and Richard A. Cloward. 1979. *Poor People's Movements: Why They Succeed, How They Fail*. New York: Vintage.

"Problems Spark Need for Island Conservation Club." 1988, 25 March. *Wallaceburg News*. 12.

"Prof. Advises Bottled Water." 1985, 4 September. *Chatham Daily News*. 10.

"Protest Planned Against Spill." 1994, 6 May. *Chatham Daily News.* 3.

"Protestors Demand Zero Spills." 1994, 13 May. *Jibkenyan.* 1.

"Public Water Meeting Draws Crowd."1985, 27 November. *Wallaceburg Courier Press.* 3.

"Rae Blasts Polluters, Backs Lake Huron Pipeline." 1986, 16 January. *Chatham Daily News.* 3.

Rogers, Raymond A. 1994. *Nature and the Crisis of Modernity: A Critique of the Contemporary Discourse on Managing the Earth.* Montreal: Black Rose.

Ross, Wayne. 1993. *Rethinking the New in New Social Movements: The St. Clair River Pollution Issue* (Unpublished Master's Thesis). Department of Political Science, Wilfred Laurier University.

Ruben, Barbara. 1993. "Protecting Mother Earth's Bottom Line." *Environmental Action.* Fall: 11–13.

Sachs, Aaron. 1995. *Eco-Justice: Linking Human Rights and the Environment.* Washington, D.C.: Worldwatch Institute.

"St. Clair: A Source of Worry for Indians." 1985, 6 September. *Jibkenyan.* 7.

"St. Clair Drinking Water Study Called Flawed and Inconclusive." 1991, 28 March. *Chatham Daily News.* 1.

"St. Clair Leakage Could Lead to Changes." 1985, 10 August. *London Free Press.* 12.

St. Clair River Area of Concern Remedial Action Plan Stage II. 1995. *Water Use Goals Remedial Measures and Implementation Strategy.* A Report by the Michigan Department of Natural Resources, Surface Water Quality Division, Planning and Special Programs Section and the Ontario Ministry of Environment and Energy, St. Clair River RAP Project.

"St. Clair River Topic of Conversation." 1985, 10 December. *Chatham Daily News.* 10.

Scarry, Elaine. 1986. *The Body in Pain: The Making and Unmaking of the World.* New York: Oxford University Press.

Schneider, Joseph W. 1985. "Social Problems Theory: The Constructionist View." *Annual Review of Sociology* 11: 209–229.

Scott, Alan. 1990. *Ideology and New Social Movements.* Winchester, Massachusetts: Unwin Hyman.

Scott, Marvin B. and Stanford M. Lyman. 1968. "Accounts." *American Sociological Review* 33: 46–62.

Sherif, William. 1936. *The Psychology of Social Norms.* New York: Harper.

Sider, Gerald. 1993. *Life Among the Lumbee.* Philadelphia: Temple University Press.

Smart, Barry. 1992. *Modern Conditions, Postmodern Controversies*. New York: Routledge.

Snow, David A. and Robert D. Benford. 1988. "Ideology, Frame Resonance, and Participant Mobilization." Pp. 197–217 in *From Structure to Action: Comparing Social Movement Research Across Cultures (International Social Movement Research 1)*, edited by Bert Klandermans, Hanspeter Kreisi, and Sidney Tarrow. Greenwich, Connecticut: JAI Press.

Snow, David A. and Robert D. Benford. 1992. "Master Frames and Cycles of Protest." Pp. 133–155 in *Frontiers in Social Movement Theory*, edited by Aldon D. Morris and Carol McClurg Mueller. New Haven, Connecticut: Yale University Press.

Snow, David A., E. Burke Rochford Jr., Steven K. Worden, and Robert D. Benford. 1986. "Frame Alignment Processes, Micromobilization, and Movement Participation." *American Sociological Review* 51: 464–481.

Snow, David A., Louis A. Zurcher Jr., and Sheldon Ekland-Olson. 1980. "Social Networks and Social Movements: A Microstructural Approach to Differential Recruitment." *American Sociological Review* 45: 787–801.

"Society Demands Stricter Controls." 1985, 9 September. *Chatham Daily News*. 5.

Spector, Malcom and John I. Kitsuse. 1987. *Constructing Social Problems*. Hawthorne, New York: Aldine de Gruyter.

Staggenborg, Suzanne. 1993. "Critical Events and the Mobilization of the Pro-Choice Movement." *Research in Political Sociology*. 6: 319–345.

Staggenborg, Suzanne. 1996. "The Survival of the Women's Movement: Turnover and Continuity in Bloomington, Indiana." *Mobilization: An International Journal of Collective Behaviour and Social Movements* 1(2) 143–158.

Stoecker, Randy. 1994. *Defending Community: The Struggle for Alternative Redevelopment in Cedar-Riverside*. Philadelphia: Temple University Press.

"Sustainable Development: What Is It?" 1991, 5 April. *Jibkenyan*. 6.

Sztompka, Piotr. 1991. *Society in Action: The Theory of Social Becoming*. Chicago: University of Chicago Press.

Sztompka, Piotr. 1993. *The Sociology of Social Change*. Cambridge, Massachusetts: Blackwell.

Tanner, Helen Hornbeck. 1987. *Atlas of Great Lakes Indian History*. Oklahoma City: University of Oklahoma Press.

Tarrow, Sidney. 1991. "Comparing Social Movement Participation in Western Europe and the United States: Problems, Uses, and a Proposal for Synthesis." Pp. 392–420 in *Research on Social Movements: The State of the Art in Western Europe and the USA,* edited by Dieter Rucht. Boulder, Colorado: Westview Press.

Tarrow, Sidney. 1992. "Mentalities, Political Cultures, and Collective Action Frames: Constructing Meaning through Action." Pp. 174–202 in *Frontiers in Social Movement Theory,* edited by Aldon D. Morris and Carol McClurg Mueller. New Haven, Connecticut: Yale University Press.

"Task Force Could Help Spills Problem." 1991, 24 July. *Wallaceburg News.* 11.

Taylor, Cynthia. 1990. "Albert Tinsley-Williams." *Environmental Action.* January/February: 25.

Taylor, D. E. 1992. "Can the Environmental Movement Attract and Maintain the Support of Minorities?" Pp. 23–45 in *Race and the Incidence of Environmental Hazards: A Time for Discourse,* edited by Bunyan Bryant and Paul Mohai. Boulder, Colorado: Westview Press.

Taylor, D. E. 1993. "Minority Environmental Activism in Britain: from Brixton to the Lake District." *Qualitative Sociology,* 16: 263–295.

Taylor, Linda. 1990. "Protect and Preserve, Or Protect and Survive." *Environmental Action.* January/February: 26–27.

Taylor, Verta and Nancy Whittier. 1992. "Collective Identity in Social Movement Communities." Pp. 98–109 in *Frontiers in Social Movement Theory,* edited by Aldon D. Morris and Carol McClurg Mueller. New Haven, Connecticut: Yale University Press.

"They Jogged to Sarnia." 1994, 27 April. *Wallaceburg News.* 6.

Tilly, Charles. 1978. *From Mobilization to Revolution.* Reading, Massachusetts: Addison-Wesley.

Tokar, Brian. 1995. "Respect Native Struggles." *Earth First!* March/April: 26.

Touraine, Alain. 1985. "An Introduction to the Study of Social Movements." *Social Research* 52: 749–787.

Touraine, Alain. 1988. *The Return of the Actor: Social Theory in Postindustrial Society.* Minneapolis: University of Minnesota Press.

Touraine, Alain. 1991. "Commentary on Dieter Rucht's Critique." Pp. 385–391 in *Research on Social Movements: The State of the Art in Western Europe and the USA,* edited by Dieter Rucht. Boulder, Colorado: Westview Press.

Touraine, Alain. 1992. "Beyond Social Movements." *Theory, Culture & Society* 9: 125–145.

Traux, Hawley. 1990. "Minorities at Risk." *Environmental Action.* January/February: 19–21.

Traux, Hawley. 1992. "Workers and Environmental Risk." *Environmental Action*. March/April: 11–13.

Trigger, Bruce. 1985. *Natives and Newcomers: Canada's "Heroic Age" Reconsidered*. Montreal/Kingston: McGill-Queen's University Press.

Trigger, David S. 1996. "Contesting Ideologies of Natural Resource Development in British Columbia, Canada." *Culture* 16: 55–67.

Turner Ralph H. 1981. "Collective Behavior and Resource Mobilization as Approaches to Social Movements: Issues and Continuities." Pp. 1–24 in *Research in Social Movements, Conflicts, and Change*, edited by Louis Krieberg. Greenwich, Connecticut: JAI Press.

Turner, Ralph H. and Lewis M. Killian. 1957. *Collective Behavior*. Englewood Cliffs, N.J.: Prentice-Hall.

"Twice-Daily Tests Show 'Burg Water Quality Good." 1986, 19 November. *Chatham Daily News*. 2.

"Unfouled Ducks Soak in River to Monitor Toxin Absorbency." 1986, 9 May. *Jibkenyan*. 4.

"Unique Air Testing Station Located on Walpole Island." 1988, 30 March. *Wallaceburg News*. 12.

"University Geneticist Critical of Wallaceburg Water Report." 1985, 18 December. *London Free Press*. 2.

VanWyck, Sheila. 1992. *Harvests Yet to Reap* (Unpublished dissertation). Department of Anthropology, University of Toronto.

VanWynsberghe, Robert. 1997. *AlterNatives: Meaning and Mobilization on Walpole Island*. (Unpublished Ph.D. dissertation). Department of Sociology, Bowling Green State University.

"Walpole and Dow Talk." 1992, 16 February. *Wallaceburg Courier Press*. 7.

"Walpole Band to Keep Its Water Intake Plant Closed." 1994, 9 February. *Sarnia News*. 10.

"Walpole Chief Lashes Out at Polluters." 1991, 19 June. *Wallaceburg News*. 2.

"Walpole Chief Wants Polysar Boss Jailed Over Latest St. Clair River Chemical Spill." 1992, 25 July. *Chatham Daily News*. 1.

"Walpole Considers Ramsar Designation." 1991, 2 May. *Chatham Daily News*. 2.

"Walpole Continues Fight Against ICI." 1995, 19 July. *Chatham Daily News*. 4.

"Walpole Decides to Pull Out of Huron Pipeline Project." 1992, 23 January. *Chatham Daily News*. 3.

"Walpole Island Band Demanding Dow Continue Water Shipments." 1994, 10 February. *London Free Press*. 4.

"Walpole Island Conservation Club Wants to Create Refuge." 1994, 25 May. *Wallaceburg Courier Press*. 3.

Walpole Island Heritage Centre Occasional Paper #6. 1985. *Walpole Island Claims Research Program: A Case Study.*

Walpole Island Heritage Centre Occasional Paper #16. 1986. *Native Community Research: A Co-Operative Approach.*

Walpole Island Heritage Centre Occasional Paper #22. 1986. *The Historical Development of the Walpole Island Community.*

Walpole Island Heritage Centre Occasional Paper #24. 1986. *A Co-Operative Study of Socio-Economic Factors in Resource Management on the Walplole Island Indian Reserve—Final Report.*

Walpole Island Heritage Centre. 1990. *Sustainable Development from an Aboriginal Perspective—An Information Package.*

Walpole Island Heritage Centre. 1995. "Environmental Issues Inventory: Phase II." Unpublished document prepared for Indian and Northern Affairs Canada.

"Walpole Island May Reject Pipeline." 1994, 26 April. *London Free Press*. 11.

"Walpole Lobbying Finally Pays Off." 1991, 21 July. *Chatham Daily News*. 3.

"Walpole Loses Bid to Halt Dredging." 1989, 27 October 27. *Jibkenyan*. 5.

"Walpole Needs Answers on Pipeline." 1991, 24 May. *Wallaceburg News*. 6.

"Walpole Seeks Native Health Study." 1992, 16 July. *Chatham Daily News*. 4.

"Walpole Still Opposes ICI." 1995, 30 May. *London Free Press*. 1.

"Walpole to Protest Incinerator." 1988, 19 February. *Jibkenyan*. 3.

"Walpole Wants Zero Spills." 1985, 11 May. *Wallaceburg Courier Press*. 1.

"Walpole Water War Continues." 1994, 12 February. *Chatham Daily News*. 7.

"Walpole's Involvement with E.A.G.L.E." 1993, 19 March. *Jibkenyan*. 2.

"War Declared on Chemical Valley." 1992, 3 April. *Jibkenyan*. 1.

"Water Contaminant Moving to Windsor." 1985, 4 September. *Chatham Daily News*. 8.

"WCCCW Off to Ottawa to Give Brief." 1988, 20 January. *Wallaceburg News*. 1.

Weinberg, Jack and Joe Thorton. 1994. "Scientific Principles." Pp. 20–26 in *Applying Weight of Evidence: Issues and Practice*, edited by Michael Gilbertson and Sally Cole-Misch. Windsor, Ontario: International Joint Commission.

"Well Injections May Have Continued." 1985, 1 November. *Chatham Daily News.* 10.

Wenz, Peter. 1988. *Environmental Justice.* Albany, N.Y.: SUNY Press.

Westra, Laura and Peter S. Wenz, eds. 1995. *Faces of Environmental Racism: Confronting Issues of Global Justice.* Lanham, Maryland: Rowan and Littlefield.

"What Is Toxic?" 1986, 7 December. *Jibkenyan.* 6.

"What We Hear, See and Think." 1992, 8 April. *Wallaceburg Courier Press.* 13.

"Why Limit Your Fish Dinner?" 1987, 22 May. *Jibkenyan.* 4.

"Williams Favors Water Tower Over Pipeline Plan for Walpole." 1991, 1 May. *Chatham Daily News.* 3.

Woolgar, Steve and Dorothy Pawluch. 1985. "Ontological Gerrymandering." *Social Problems* 32: 214–227.

Wuthnow, Robert. 1989. *Communities of Discourse: Ideology and Social Structure in the Reformation, the Enlightenment, and European Socialism.* Cambridge, Massachusetts: Harvard University Press.

Yin, Robert. 1994. *Case Study Research: Design and Methods.* Thousand Oaks, California: Sage.

Zald, Mayer N. 1991. "The Continuing Vitality of Resource Mobilization Theory, a Response to Herbert Kitschelt's Critique." Pp. 348–354 in *Research on Social Movements: The State of the Art in Western Europe and the USA,* edited by Dieter Rucht. Boulder, Colorado: Westview Press.

Zald, Mayer N. and Roberta Ash. 1966. "New Social Movement Organizations: Growth, Decay and Change." *Social Forces* 44: 327–441.

Zald, Mayer N. and John McCarthy. 1987. *Social Movements in an Organizational Society.* New Brunswick, N.J.: Transaction Publishers.

"Zero Discharge." 1992, 29 May. *Jibkenyan.* 1.

Index

Fire, 45, 98
First Fire, 45
Frame alignment, 20, 111
Frame bridging, 96, 109–110
Framing, 87
Free passage, right of, 11
Friends of the United Nations, 34
Fur trade, 46, 66

Garbage imperialism, xii
Gas pipeline, 53
Genocide, cultural, xii, 26
Global Action Plan for the Earth, 69
Global Rivers Environmental
    Education Network
    (GREEN), 33, 69
Grassroots activism, 12, 107
GREEN. See Global Rivers
    Environmental Education
    Network.
Green community identity, 19
Greeness, 57
Green movement, 20–21
Greenpeace, 42

Health studies, birth defects
    study (1986), 68, 79n, 86
Heritage Centre
    (Nin.da.waab.jig) (formerly
    Research Group), xi, 16, 18,
    20, 27, 28–39, 99n
    building, 28
    collective action frame of
        ecological Native/sustain-
        able community, 21, 88, 89,
        93, 95, 100, 112
    collective action frame's
        cultural boundaries, 88
    community opposition
        response, 85–87
    criticism, 35–36
    employees, 28, 75, 76
    funding, 28
    internal publications, 26, 29
    lack of respect for, 34–35

location, 28
organizational plan, 30
purpose, 34
recruitment, 47
reformulation of collective
    action frame, 100–102
reformulation of sustain-
    ability, 67–69
special interest groups, 38
support of collective activity, 22
wild meat survey, 59
women's circle, 37
Highbanks, 28
Historical nodal point, 23
History of Walpole Island, 3–8,
    63–67, 81–85
Household hazardous waste
    depot, 69
Huron nation, 46, 65
Husserlian lifeworld, 20
Hydro line, 33, 53

Imperial Chemical Industries of
    Canada (ICI), 89–103, 89n
    Management Plan, 103
Indian Act (1876), 3–4, 3n, 5, 85
    Bill C-31 amendment, 4–5
Indian Agent, 6, 7, 84
    removal of, 26–27
Indian nations, recognition of, 26
Indian Removal Act (1830), 64, 81
Indian Territory, establishment
    of, 64
Indigenous peoples, vii
International Joint Commission,
    43, 93
Iron Eyes Cody, xiv, 52, 53
Iroquois, 46, 47

Jibkenyan (community newspa-
    per), 32, 43, 49, 74, 94, 95

Lake Ontario agreement, 65
Land Claims Office, 27
Leasing of land, 5, 7
Legal Natives, 4